Everlasting
Motherhood

Other books by Emma Heaphy

Dear Motherhood
Mother On
Motherhood to Me

Everlasting Motherhood

Poetry and prose about the experience of early motherhood
with a last baby, with older babies growing up,
and of middle motherhood knocking on the door.

With empathy
EMMA HEAPHY

Copyright © Emma Heaphy 2025

First published 2025

All rights reserved

No part of this book may be reproduced or transmitted in any form or by any means, electronic or mechanical, including photocopying, recording or by any information storage and retrieval system, without prior permission in writing from the publisher.

A catalogue record for this book is available from the National Library of New Zealand.

Soft cover ISBN 978-0-473-74659-9
Kindle ISBN 978-1-0670823-0-7
epub ISBN 978-1-0670823-1-4

Design & layout www.yourbooks.co.nz

This book is dedicated to my husband,
and our four beautiful children who are my everlasting.

Remember –
the sky is your limit.
So, I will be there,
even after my life has reached its own –
helping you to reach the stars.

Contents

Introduction 1

CHAPTER ONE: PREGNANCY 3
    Our little secret 4
    Working miracles 6
    Opportunity 8
    Like glue 9
    Not me 10
    More than once 11
    Childhoods intertwined 13
    Last pregnancy 14
    Knowing 16
    What to expect 17
    A future message from your baby 19

CHAPTER TWO: LOSS 21
    Due date 22
    In good hands 23

CHAPTER THREE: POSTPARTUM 24
    My era 25
    Day by day 26
    Entire world 28
    A home 30
    All that love 31
    A message from your new baby 32
    Real life 33
    Postpartum Partner 34
    Friends, family, everyone else 36
    Myself 37
    Completely complete 38

Chapter Four: Tired 40
- Chosen one 41
- Her tired 42
- Leader 43
- Driver 45
- Strongest woman 46

Chapter Five: Mothering Multiple Children 48
- Pending Mother of Three (or more)... 49
- Number four 51
- Middle children 52
- Doing it 53
- Teammates 55
- Busy 56
- Togetherness 58
- Been and gone 59

Chapter Six: Physical Load 60
- Slowing 61
- Love language 63
- Does it really matter? 65
- Reframe 66
- Selfish 67
- Unfinished business 68

Chapter Seven: Mental Load 69
- "Mum will know" 70
- Overstimulated 71
- Everything else 72
- Break 73
- Alone 74
- Queen 75

CHAPTER EIGHT: TIME IN IMPORTANT WORK 76
    What a SAHM needs..77
    SAHM salary..78
    Time in..80
    Bonus..82
    String to her bow 83
    Workforce application letter..84

CHAPTER NINE: DAY IN MY LIFE 86
    Master of one...87
    High-functioning...88
    Always something..89
    Nervous system..90
    Alone time 91
    More to lose...92
    My life 93
    One more day 94

CHAPTER TEN: SPECIAL OCCASION................................ 96
    Currency..97
    Wish list 98
    Magic master 99
    Credit 100
    Mother's Day 101
    Motherhood occasion 102

CHAPTER ELEVEN: STRUGGLING 103
    Groundhog Day..104
    Contradictions 105
    What I really mean 107
    Signs 109
    Differences..110
    Ups and downs...111

    Masking.. 112
    Same same 113
    What you are 114
    Breathe.. 115
    Eventually 116

Chapter Twelve: Friendships 117
    What's it like? 118
    Next time... 120
    More than me 122
    That friend 124

Chapter Thirteen: Marriage 125
    Dad... 126
    Wearing motherhood 127
    Roommates... 129
    Hand in hand 131
    Needs... 132
    Team... 133
    Best day(s) of my life 134
    Snip 135
    Dear Husband 137

Chapter Fourteen: Growing Pains 138
    I get it now
    (last baby edition) 139
    They were right 140
    Finality 142
    Without warning 143
    Shadows.. 144
    Five 145
    Six 147
    More than mum 149
    Loving you today 152

Chapter Fifteen: Raising Siblings 153
- Sunrise 154
- Sisterhood 156
- Older siblings 157
- Younger siblings 158
- Sons 160
- Daughters 161
- Continues with them 162

Chapter Sixteen: Raising Myself 163
- More than myself 164
- Fun Mum 165
- "Normal" 166
- Light 167
- My needs 168
- Stop/start 169
- Wealth 170
- Something special 171
- Future version 172
- Mother 173

Chapter Seventeen: Growing Gains 174
- Farewell 175
- Hard truth 177
- New meaning 178
- Afterwards 180
- Me to you 181
- Cool Mum 182
- All grown up 184
- Gift 185
- Reminders that stand the test of time: 186

CHAPTER EIGHTEEN: LOOKING BACK..........................187
    The chance... 188
    Speed of time 190
    This too shall pass 191
    Would I? 192
    Made to last 193
    POV: They're no longer little..................................... 195
    Unstoppable.. 197
    Knowing... 198

CHAPTER NINETEEN:
EVERLASTING MOTHERHOOD..199
    Opportunity 200
    Always 202
    Forever home 203
    Stay...205
    Destination heart 206
    Take a bow..207
    My children 208
    Best parts..209
    Until the end.. 210
    Remember when 211

Introduction

I'm so glad you are here. Maybe you have come from my earlier books. Maybe this is your first experience with my writing. Either way, I want you to know you are welcome within these pages. And I'd love for you to stay.

My first book, *Dear Motherhood* is about new motherhood. The two that follow, *Mother On* and *Motherhood to Me*, cover the ups and downs of continued early motherhood as I transitioned from one-to-two, and then two-to-three, children. This collection, *Everlasting Motherhood* picks up where we left off. We just add in one more baby, who happens to be my last. This book dives deeper into life as a growing family, taps into those last baby feels during the first year with the new addition, and offers empathetic perspectives about the move towards middle motherhood on the horizon.

May this book give you the courage to face the lasts, and to continue embracing them as time moves too quickly. May it give you the hope you need to see that motherhood doesn't end with your last baby, even though there can be many concluding factors you are faced with. And may it give words to your feelings, and a voice to your heart when everything feels overwhelming – not just with your last baby, but with those other babies of yours who are getting bigger and older and need different things.

I hope these poems make you really feel something.

With empathy,

Emma Heaphy xxx

Starting point

Maybe you think you are done with having children but are not sure you are ready to be done, and so you spend so much time considering whether you are done.

Maybe you are done, and know you need to be done but still feel so emotional about being done.

Maybe you are done and are 100% ready to be done and cannot wait to be in the next stage already.

Maybe you are not done but have to be done and struggle to come to terms with being done before you are ready to be.

Or maybe you have not even started and will forever be wondering what both "begun" and "done" feel like.

The motherhood experience is complex and nuanced.
We all have different feelings at every stage.
And no single feeling is the right one.

Remember –
It's okay to let yourself run away with whatever makes you feel closest with your authenticity.
It's your motherhood.
And no one else can tell you how you should feel in it.

CHAPTER ONE

PREGNANCY

"I'll never have to do this again" verses "I'll never get to do this again" is the push/pull of last pregnancy emotions.

Our little secret

It's been our little secret,
from the moment I saw two lines.
You and I together,
for a special little time.

I wear the baggy shirts,
and very much lay low,
feeling a little worse for wear
as I grow your fingers and toes.

I skip the social events,
or delay them until next time.
And then say "no thanks" to scallops,
and turn down a glass of wine.

I eat like crazy in private.
The cravings are always strong.
Hiding the dead giveaway,
I'll be unable to be before long.

I talk about you often,
with the very few I've told.
You are all I think about
as the weeks continue to unfold.

The ultrasound arrives.
And nerves consume every part
of the body we have shared as one
from the very early start.

Chapter One

Thankfully it goes our way,
and relief enters the room.
The secret that's been us for weeks,
is a story ready to bloom.

I'm so excited to share it.
But part of me wants to wait,
to let others be part of
our everyday blind date.

Although when I tell them,
I know how loved you'll be.
It's our little secret now,
and a huge deal, really.

There's just something about knowing,
when others haven't a clue,
whether we're "finding out",
or when exactly you're due.

We get this special time,
even though it can be tough.
And seeing that has helped me through
the hardest of the rough.

So let's just be in it,
the secret only we know.
For it's the start of a lifetime
of sharing how we both grow.

Working miracles

I just want to rest –
But I have dinner to make,
and dishes to clean from lunch.

I just want to rest –
But if I put off the washing again today,
the uniforms won't be clean for tomorrow.

I just want to rest –
But I have emails to respond to,
and appointments to organise.

I just want to rest –
But I need to connect with my children,
and the homework won't do itself.

Chapter One

I just want to rest,
my body needs rest,
but the rest is history,
because some things can't wait.

So, I wait.
And wait.
Unrested,
but powerful.

I wait.
And wait.
Working miracles,
while growing one.

Opportunity

This is a once in a last-time opportunity.
I get to grow life here – in this tired, stretched
but incredible body of mine.
Not everyone can.
I think about that often, especially in the tough moments.

It doesn't seem fair.
Everyone should get the chance to experience this
if they choose to.
It doesn't seem fair that the journey for some into it,
or through it, can be so damn hard.

I get to do this.
I can do this.
I am tired, stretched but so incredibly lucky.

This is my last-time opportunity.
I know that.
So with every tired, stretched,
and incredibly hard moment –
I will let myself feel as I need to,
but I won't let myself forget what I have.

CHAPTER ONE

Like glue

Some will ask you –
"How many have you got in there?"

Some will tell you –
"You must be due soon".

Some will remind you –
"They've got to come out somehow".

While others will simply say –
"You are glowing".
"I hope you are doing okay".
"What an exciting time for your family".

And sadly, it's amazing what sticks more.

*(Not commenting on people's bodies
applies to pregnant women too).*

not me

"What's going on?"
I ask myself
as I try to go with the flow.

My big bump reminds me
I'm blessed with this life
but I can't see my glow.

I'm hormonal, deflated,
restless, overstimulated,
my body is not what I know.

It's fragile, and stretched,
exhausted, unkempt,
struggling to take it slow.

I'm grumpy, defeated,
feel frumpy and overheated,
I don't feel myself as I grow.

But I need to remember
as I face this dilemma –
It's pregnancy,
not the me I know.

Chapter One

More than once

In past pregnancies I have been in a state of panic
by this point.
I've wanted everything sorted by the time the baby is here.
I've worried about whether my children would be okay
without me at night, and not just when I'm away from
them giving birth, but for the early postpartum period too.
I've stressed over what I still need to get "perfect" to
make the transition as easy as possible for everyone,
including myself.
But what I've learnt now, having done this more than once,
and knowing I may not get to do this again, is this –
My children will be okay without me for a while.
And if they are not, it is only temporary.
They will see it was all worth it after only a short while of
distress.
We have more time to make up for all the cuddles,
and we will have a bigger family to hug.
They will sleep through the night when they are all ready,
and I can handle a newborn waking at night with others too.
My husband and I will always make it work.
We have done it in the past, and we will again.
There is nothing we can't do as a team.
The cot doesn't need to be made up before birth.
The clothing doesn't need to be perfectly folded in the
drawers.

Everlasting Motherhood

And the world won't end if the nursery paintings aren't hung
for when we get home.
We have more time.
For me, pregnancy at the end feels harder than those
first weeks postpartum.
And when I'm in the first weeks postpartum,
it feels harder than pregnancy.
I need to get through each stage as I'm in them,
not worry about what comes next.
And then in the moments I can enjoy the present,
really savour them.
They won't last forever.
But also, forever won't last.
And lastly, I can do it.
I will do it.
I know nothing will be perfect, but everything will be okay.
For my children,
I will always make sure of it.

CHAPTER ONE

Childhoods intertwined

I'm bringing out the baby clothes again.
There's something so special about it.
I hold them up and see how small they are,
then bring them close to my body
to feel how real this is becoming.
My older children were once here
inside these tiny pieces of cloth.
Soon my youngest will be too.
And one day we will look back at the photos
of them wearing some of the same small pieces
at different times –
A reminder of childhoods intertwined,
not only by memories shared,
but by hand-me-downs too.

Last pregnancy

Your last pregnancy can be the hardest.
Not just because of the physical aspects,
like your older children that you have to look after
while pregnant.
Or even your morning sickness.
But also because of the emotional aspects,
like knowing you will never experience
growing life again,
or have your children live through it with you.
Every day is one day closer to meeting the end of the hard.
But also one day closer to never having
any of the beauty again.
Each next step forward is a last, of this type.
You are sentimental.
Often emotional.
But too busy to let yourself feel it.
Until you feel it all at once in the middle of some realisation
that you will never have this again.
Your body is a temple of gratitude and grief.
Nothing makes you feel luckier.
But also, at times, everything makes you sad
about what you will never get to relive.
You have seen so much strength through times
already passed.

CHAPTER ONE

Through previous pregnancies,
and the children you already have.
But it's difficult to see this time,
when you feel as fragile as that tiny growing baby
inside of you.
Last pregnancies are filled with complicated feelings.
So many feelings.
And there's something about looking at your bump
this time around that seems to make that
really hit home.
So, as you glance at the body you once didn't know,
you hold space for the feelings you couldn't prepare for
and wait as patiently as you ever have for
the baby you are yet to meet.
Because knowing that this is the last time
you will ever feel this exact way,
and this type of hard,
makes it easier too.

Knowing

I'm excited for birth again, and I'm nervous.
I can't wait for postpartum again, and I can.
I'm looking forward to having my body back again,
and I'm already mourning my bump.
This is what it is to go back into this,
knowing what it can be like already.
Knowledge is power,
but it can also feel like a weakness here.
You can, and you can't.
You will, and you won't.
The nerves are hungry, so you feed them
with all you've been through before.
I don't know if it makes it harder, this knowing.
But you do remember it's worth it too.
And in this middle ground,
I guess that's the most important thing to feed yourself.

CHAPTER ONE

What to expect

Pregnant with your last baby?
Let me hold you while I say this…

You will cry when you least expect over times already gone.
You will hold onto things that serve no purpose
other than to balm your breaking heart.
You will say "please don't grow up too fast" over and over.
You will let yourself get more overstimulated.
You will let yourself get more touched out.
You will let yourself get more tired if it means
you get to be in the fleeting moment that little bit longer.
You will be out of your comfort zone, again.
You will evolve, again.
And you will have to dig deep out of the brokenness
that comes with loosening your grip.

You will have your last baby and see that the firsts
of new motherhood were really testing you for this.

It's emotionally challenging here, even if you know for sure
it's your last, and that's been the plan all along.

Everlasting Motherhood

But let me say this too —

You will start to see a newer motherhood through the
lens of a version of you who must say farewell to a huge part
of what you've come to know in yourself, and your children,
before you're ready.
And that gives you the fresh start you didn't know
you needed.

You will be okay.
Better even, eventually.
Because what you face will be challenging,
but what you're building is everlasting.
And it takes time to really see that.

Chapter One

A future message from your baby

We made it.
You are holding me in your arms like we both
dreamed for all those months.
And you are as perfect as I imagined.

You stare at me often.
And although my vision isn't crystal clear just yet,
your voice and touch is all I need.
That's all I remember from the inside anyway.

I used to listen to everything, you know.
When I wasn't sleeping, that is.
I know growing me wasn't easy.
I heard you cry sometimes, and talk to dad
about the tougher times you went through
to grow me big and strong.
I felt it sometimes – your pain and trying.
Your body doesn't lie.

But I also felt the easier moments too.
Like the first time on the ultrasound
(sorry I moved too much).
And every time I touched your hand from the inside
(I loved that too).

Back then, all I wanted was to tell you
"I'm here. I'm real. And I can't wait to meet you.
I just need some more time".
Because I knew you needed to hear that and feel it.
But today all of that seems like a distant memory.
A means to a beautiful end and an exciting new beginning.

Because of you, everything worked out.
Thank you for everything.
I loved you from the very start.

CHAPTER TWO

LOSS

*No one feels it the way you do
because no one loved them exactly the way you do.*

Due date

Your due date is today,
but you are not here.
Another year has gone by without you in my arms,
or in the nursery I envisaged,
or at the table with your brothers and sisters
like I so often dreamed.
I think of you often, you know.
All days,
but particularly today.
You were meant to be here,
but on that day those few years ago,
we lost you early,
in what will always be a forever too soon.

Chapter Two

In good hands

I'm in heaven,
and it's beautiful here.
There are mothers, fathers, aunties, uncles
and grandparents everywhere.
They rock me to sleep, play with me
and cuddle me whenever I want.
And that's a lot, because I miss you so much.
But I'm okay, I promise.
There are so many familiar faces.
They tell me they were close with you.
Now they are close to me.
Actually, they look out for me most.
There are other children up here too.
They share their toys with me,
and make sure I never feel left out.
All these special people –
they tell me they are looking after me
until you get here one day.
I can't wait for that day.
But I'm in good hands in the meantime, Mum.
I promise.

CHAPTER THREE

POSTPARTUM

One of the best gifts you can give a newly postpartum mother who has children already is anything that can make her feel something close to being that brand new postpartum mother again. Because the postpartum experience changes the more children she has. But she's still that brand new mother with her brand-new baby, really.

Chapter Three

My era

I'm in my "last baby" era.
My "everything is particularly emotional,
sentimental and purposeful" one.
And not only with my last baby,
but with my older babies, too.
With this, I now know –
Your first baby gives you a life-changing perspective.
Your last baby gives you a motherhood-changing one.

Day by day

Postpartum is forever.
Early postpartum is day by day.
In this fresh season of newborn life,
almost every moment is new and different,
messy and chaotic.
All you know is that you will be needed (at all times),
you will have almost no sleep (when you need it),
and you will have fallen deeply in love (once again).
The rest is yet to be figured out,
because today won't look like tomorrow
and tomorrow won't look like next week.
You need to find your rhythm –
Any sort of rhythm –
But you have to wade through so many things beforehand.
The endless nappies – yours included.
Your sore body – that needs rest while still sustaining new
life, and those lives you brought into the world beforehand.
The night shifts – that bring so much inner joy
and outward pain.

Chapter Three

Your emotions – coming in like waves
that don't know how to wait their turns.
And all this while, trying to soak up every second
of your new baby, your changing body, and your family life
which isn't the same as it was – just better.
This stage is intense in almost every way.
It leaves you weak, and strong, deprived and empowered,
so broken and so in love.
Postpartum is forever.
But for this period in the fog –
When you don't know what day it is,
how many times you woke last night
or what side they last fed from –
It's mostly about taking it day by day.

Entire world

What I mean when I say "I've just had a baby"...

I've never been on such a high, but my body feels broken right now. It needs so much rest and healing, time and grace. Sometimes I forget I've grown this entire being from scratch.

I think about how many women carry on after having a baby as if we haven't – a reminder that what you see isn't always the measure of what someone's been through. Pregnancy and postpartum becomes invisible.

It's like I've known my baby forever. But it's also like I'm meeting myself again. And not the woman I once knew, but the re-formed one. The one who looks pregnant when she no longer is. The one who is layered in tired. The one who looks like she's just given birth but hasn't figured it all out just yet.

CHAPTER THREE

I stare at my baby after every blink, but the nights are not always my friend. My baby needs me to be awake often, but I'm a human who needs sleep, and a mother of older children who also depend on me. I am in survival mode, constantly.

I've never been so depended on. I am my baby's lifeline. But I've also never been so dependent on all support, particularly from my husband. We have been brought closer than ever through all of this but sometimes finding the "us" in "all of us" takes work.

My house is a mess. My mind is a mess. I am often
a mess. I'm overstimulated. I'm under stimulated.
I see red and feel beige and I've never cried this much.

But I'm doing it. I'm getting through the harder moments, riding through the easier ones, and loving through it all.

Because "I've just had a baby",
but I've also got my entire world in my arms.

A home

My children see my body for what it is.
Flesh.
Bone.
Their home.

They don't pick it apart.
They love it.
Need it.
From the very start.

My body isn't what I see.
No.
My eyes and mind –
They play tricks on me.

My body –
It's more than some reflection.
It's given me them.
And they are my life.
So, at the very least,
It deserves my affection.

Chapter Three

All that love

A baby will make you realise –
How loved you are, and how tired you are.
How soft you are, and how strong you can be.
How much you are needed, and how much you need.
How far you would go, and how little you really know.
How much time you don't have,
and how many important things you do.
How happy you can be, and how low some days find you.
How perfect you are to someone,
and how much you need to work on for them.
A baby will make you realise things you never
knew about yourself,
but that you really needed to know,
and take all of that, and love you for it.
Because you are their realisation,
every day,
of what it is to be loved.

A message from your new baby

I wake and slowly open my eyes.
I can't see much yet.
I move my head from side to side
and stretch out my scrunched body.
Am I where I think I am?
I check for your softness beneath me,
your scent above me,
and your touch around me.
You're here.
I'm home.
And so my heart rate slows.
I nuzzle close into you to fill my tummy
with your warm milk.
I don't taste your tired, or depletion – just your love.
My eyes start to feel heavy again
as I am living in my own dream awake.
"You are heaven. I can't wait to see you here again soon"
I think, as I fall into a deep sleep, knowing –
There is nowhere I would rather be.

CHAPTER THREE

Real life

I scroll across every line on your face.
I heart every little corner of your smile.
I swipe the tears of disbelief off my cheeks
as I look at you existing in your tiny body
on my chest.
"Sometimes I wish social media wasn't real",
I comment to myself.
Because you are.
And spending my time on you
makes me feel so much better.

Postpartum Partner

Bare minimum things that can make a huge difference postpartum:

Asking her how her night was if you didn't get up with the baby. She needs her hard work at night to be acknowledged too.

Playing with any older children (outside if possible) for a while when you get home. Trust me, she needs it. (Added points for asking whether she wants you to take the baby too.)

If you take the baby or other children to give her a "break" (aka a shower, a meal, or some other basic need she's been deprived of) unless there's an emergency, don't bring them back until she's had at least some time.

CHAPTER THREE

Tell her you love her and appreciate all she has done to bring your baby into the world. Know that when she looks at her new reflection, she needs to hear that more than she cares to admit. *Warning: she may cry.*

Keep asking her what you can do to help, especially when she's feeding the baby. If she says "no" or "I can't think of anything right now", find something that needs doing and do it. She'll notice and appreciate it. Her mind can't keep up with everything and needs decluttering.

Be gentle with her. Give grace often. Be the softness she needs right now. She loves and appreciates you – So much more than the bare minimum.

Friends, family, everyone else

I want to be there.
I want to do the thing.
I want to see you again.
And I would, if I could.
But I can't right now,
because I am deep in early motherhood.
And that's a reason, not an excuse.

CHAPTER THREE

Myself

I am a walking IOU.
I have been pregnant, breastfeeding
or postpartum back-to-back for years.
I have been sleep-deprived for years.
I have been hanging by a thread
physically and mentally for years,
with the thread holding me together
being the family I have created because of it all.
And there will be no more babies now,
as sad as that still feels some days.
But as my body starts to recognise itself again,
as I start to feel somewhat balanced,
as I can begin to remember what a full night's sleep is again,
and how I feel when I have time to eat proper food again,
and what it is to sit down from time to time again –
I will give myself grace,
I will take things slowly,
I will let myself enjoy the recovery process.
Because I am indebted to myself for everything
I have given over the last few years.
And I owe it to every previous version of me
to repay that debt in full.

Completely complete

If you asked me when I wasn't sure –
I would have said I don't think I'll ever feel done
having babies.
There was still that longing to have it all once again.
The newborn scent.
The toddler cuddles.
The chats with my school-aged children.
Even if it meant going through another pregnancy,
and the hard moments that come with a life of postpartum.
Even if I needed to be done, but wasn't feeling done.
Even if there was still an "if" or "but",
I would have always wondered and hoped
for more than maybe.
Because even if I said I was "done",
I wouldn't have got to the "complete" feeling.

CHAPTER THREE

But if you asked me when I was sure –
I would tell you that my last baby is my last baby.
Maybe with tears in my eyes.
Maybe not.
It depends on how I feel that day.
I would tell you that I still want to hold babies,
be held by toddlers and be amused by childhood chats,
but that I feel ready for all of that to come from
my friends' babies or those of my children
(if they have their own someday).
I would tell you that completeness has come.
And by that I mean the longing for another
doesn't keep me up at night, and the wondering is no longer.
I see my family in the future –
And it's the same, just older and wiser.
It's bigger in love, but not in number.
I would tell you I didn't ever know I'd get here.
Or when.
But I am now.
I'm completely content.
And finally –
I feel completely complete.

CHAPTER FOUR

TIRED

To me, the nights of broken sleep can be exhausting.
To my baby, the nights of waking to me are heavenly.
I know my tired body heals little hearts.
And I've never been so willing to be so exhausted.

Chapter Four

Chosen one

I often think of babies who want to be rocked and held.
Who want to be close to their mothers or fathers.
The babies who don't go into their cribs easily.
Who don't allow you to be a list-ticker.
The babies who need to be in a carrier
and cry when you leave the room.
I think that these babies are sending a message.
A message that you need to slow down.
That you need to take a breath.
That you need to just be in the moments with them.
I think these babies come into our lives at a time where
we need reminding of what is really important in life.
Because with these babies –
It's easy to feel unproductive.
It's easy to feel like everything else is falling to the wayside.
It's easy to feel touched out but also
out of touch with what matters most in the moment –
The slowing down when you can.
The riding out the hard moments.
And the trying, desperately,
to enjoy the closeness and dependence they have on you
for this small period in your life.
I think these babies choose us for a reason.
And we need to try and embrace being the chosen ones,
while we are just that.

Her tired

You can think she looks tired,
but you can never truly know how tired she is.
And weirdly enough, neither does she.
It's almost like she's gotten used to it now.
It's like she's forgotten what it felt like to be properly rested so
she gaslights herself into thinking she can operate
at the same level as the one who is,
no matter how unhealthy that is.
This is the depths of a mother's exhaustion.
A beyond the surface, bone-deep, unrecognisable beast.
Please be gracious with her.
Everything in motherhood is easier with sleep.
And sleep is only part of it.

CHAPTER FOUR

Leader

We've woken, and things aren't working properly.
The dynamics are a little off between us.
I'm tired.
We all are.
I've not managed to have breakfast,
and they haven't eaten theirs.
I've not gotten myself out of my pjs,
and they are refusing to wear warm clothes.
I've not done the dishes from last night,
and they don't know where to start with play.
They are looking to me for guidance,
even though it's not always easy to see today.
They need me to lead the way.
So I leave everything else, and try something new.
Because when nothing else is working,
something has to change.
Because when they are so young,
someone else has to show them that.

Everlasting Motherhood

So we go outside.
And eventually everything changes.
As is turns out, fresh air
and having our feet touch the grass is all we've needed.
This is the family dynamic we all were trying for,
but couldn't get earlier.
And perhaps this is the real parenting flex –
showing them healthy coping mechanisms
when everything feels impossibly hard,
and being the one to take the lead for us all.
Because maybe one day they'll know to do the same
for themselves when things aren't working,
all because of the times their parents tried to show
them the way in their own moments of feeling like
everything is just that impossibly hard.

CHAPTER FOUR

Driver

You were made for motherhood.
For all of its twists and turns.
For all of its roundabouts that can make you feel
like you are driving nowhere.
You have it in you to do this.
To get up today and drive.
You will do this.
You will keep your foot on the pedal,
even when your light isn't showing green.
Because you know your children need you.
And through motherhood you make yourself strong.

Strongest woman

When my last baby starts sleeping through,
I will think of her.
Of the version of me who was stuck in zombie mode
day in day out until I forgot what day it was.
The one who knew the way around the house in darkness
like the back of her hand, and got up time and time again,
when she felt like she couldn't.
The one who relied heavily on coffee,
and her husband's shoulder when it all got too much.
The version of me who pushed through pain
and exhaustion to sustain life.
The one who in one moment loved being an entire universe,
and in the next didn't want to be touched for one
more second.
The version who sat in the same old rocking chair,
in her old maternity wear, trying to soak up another
love of her life while thinking about everything else
that still needed to be done or how late she was
to something.

Chapter Four

I will look back at photos of when she was in the thick of sleep deprivation. I'll see how much resilience and determination she showed when being this tired felt like her entire personality. And I'll take particular notice of how content she looked despite the bags under her eyes and the stains on her clothes. I'll be so proud that she took the photos anyway.
When I get to this moment, I won't forget this version of me.
She was the one who carried me through the darkness with each of my children.
The one who didn't stop until she found the light.
She is the strongest woman I've ever known.
And I'm so proud to call her part of me.

CHAPTER FIVE

MOTHERING MULTIPLE CHILDREN

The first child gets the fresh new mother.
The middle children get the more balanced and experienced mother.
And the last child gets the worldly and sentimental one.
Every child gets a different version of their mother depending on where they come in the family.
But regardless of where they come,
They all get the same amount of love.

CHAPTER FIVE

Pending Mother of Three (or more)...

Things are about to change in a big, and beautiful way.
They say you will be outnumbered.
And at times you will be.
You don't have enough hands.
And your arms may often be too heavy.
Someone almost always has to wait.
And waiting for yourself becomes even more common,
with the times you get back to yourself fewer
and farther in between.
There will be pairings, and someone feeling left out.
There will be more mess, and less time to clean it.
There will be jumping back and forth between
different ages and stages, rooms and beds
and there will be times where you feel like
you're not enough.
Because how can one person be there for all three,
or four, or more?
But you can.
And you are.

Everlasting Motherhood

It's just not always obvious.
You meet them where they are.
And when you can't straight away,
you meet them eventually.
Because things take longer here.
There is much more room for error.
And more grace is required.
But you have enough room to grow.
You grow like your family.
You get to watch two or more older children
become older siblings – simultaneously.
You get to trust that you and your husband
can lean into each other with all of your collective weight
without falling over.
Suddenly your family feels huge,
even though it didn't happen overnight.
And nothing feels more fitting,
even though the days can feel like one big jumble.
There is a whole new life waiting for you.
And when you find your feet you don't stop running.
Because this new life you share with many
becomes the best thing to ever happen to you all.

Chapter Five

number four

They say the fourth child doesn't make much of a difference,
as you are already used to the chaos.
But you made all the difference.
You confirmed I can do it, all over again.
And that every part of it was worth it.
You were the evenness in number,
but also in my mothering.
You have softened my rough edges
by giving me a reason to give myself grace.
And without knowing it,
you have been my gentle place to land.
I guess that's what happens when you've been here before,
in what now feels to be the perfect number of times.
You didn't get the brand new mother,
the rearranged mother of two,
or the evolving and outnumbered mother of three.
You got a mix of them all with a pinch of experience.
And you are the experience.
You have grounded me.
You have stabilised me.
Your existence has brought everything into balance.
You are the one we went for after the fullness
of the others who came before you.
You are my one of four.
My number four.
And every fraction of me feels the difference
you have made to our family already.

Middle children

You're my middle.
My in-between.
My not-first-or-last.
But you are also the centre of my universe.
You have me, completely.
Even when you feel lost in it all.
When I'm with the baby,
who needs me so much right now,
or with the oldest,
who communicates more easily than you –
know I'm here for you too.
For you are still my baby, just in a bigger body.
You are still my number one, just with a different birthday.
And when others seem to pay more attention
to those on either side of you,
try not to pay attention to that.
You are not less worthy, or less important.
You are deserving of what those surrounding you get, too.
You are my middle.
My centre.
One of my main characters.
You are a piece of my puzzle that will never be lost,
or rearranged, even when things around you change.
You will always be my middle.
And I would be completely lost without you.
We all would be.

CHAPTER FIVE

Doing it

"I don't know how you do it", they say,
as they see my children hanging off me.

And what I want to tell them is –

"Because I see them playing together,
sharing with each other or cuddling on the couch
and everything hard goes out the window,
and I can only view how amazing our life together is
right now".

"Because my husband and I glance over
at each other sometimes while they include us
in their wholesome chaos, and we give each other
a little smile of knowing that we are living
the best days of our lives".

Everlasting Motherhood

"Because I don't just see them at this age.
I see them growing up together.
I see them working through hard things together.
I see them leaning on each other,
celebrating each other, learning from each other,
and sharing stories of this time over and over
for the rest of their lives".

"Because I am tired. And imperfect.
And not the A-type mother I thought I would be.
But I have them. And they have shown me
more about myself than anyone else.
They have given me the strength to keep going.
They are my how, what, when and why".

But I don't.
Instead, I tell them "I'm not sure either", with a laugh.
Because the truth is,
with said children hanging off me,
I really don't have the time.

CHAPTER FIVE

Teammates

It's easy to feel defeated.
By a baby not sleeping through yet.
A toddler not eating dinner again.
Or a school kid waiting until the last minute
to get ready every morning.
And it's hard to keep going on feeling that way.
But our children are not here to defeat us.
They are here to learn.
So, we accept the challenges.
Decide the battles which are not worth fighting,
And remember –
We are the team leaders
at a time when our teammates need us most.

Busy

If you asked me how it's going with young children
I'd say…
"I'm busy, that's for sure".

But if you saw the inside of my house,
you'd really see that.
There are washing piles I'm not sure I'll get to.
Random toys on the bathroom floor.
And there is no room left on the fridge for notices,
photos, or artwork.

My car would also tell that story.
There are crumbs between seats.
A floor covered with drink bottles and hats.
And a boot filled with the emergency essentials,
which I dig into almost daily.

And then there's my mind.
Trust me when I say it's a minefield.
A never ending up and down.
A round and round cluster of thoughts and feelings.
Battles and wins.
It's steps ahead because everyone depends on it.
But it's behind in rest, and is tired.
So tired.
The guilt for everything is exhausting.
It even makes the sleep deprivation
feel manageable sometimes.

Chapter Five

You don't see all of this unless I show you or tell you,
in intricate detail.
What you see is my children.
With all they need.
In love. Support. Each other.
Because they have that.
I make sure of it.
I love them, in everything I do.
In every little detail.
In every one of them.

They are my life.
These four beautiful souls.
And I would do anything for them.

"I'm busy", I'd say.
But I guess what I really mean is…
"I'm busy in love. That's for sure".

Togetherness

We have a whole-house family.
The children play in every room including their rooms,
our room, the living room, kitchen, and bathrooms.
They sleep and rest in rooms that are not their own, too.
They play where we are.
They often sleep where we are.
They spend time where we are.
Our house is filled with shared spaces.
A home of togetherness.
And I wouldn't have it any other way.

Chapter Five

Been and gone

I'm a mother of children close in age.
And what I will never be prepared for
is how quickly the firsts and lasts come and go.
Everything is on fast-forward as you are asked
to survive and thrive in such a short space of time.
You watch them grow up, one right after the other.
Suddenly you have new milestones that creep up on you
and lasts that you don't have time to process in fullness.
And you are only ever stopped in your tracks
when your youngest, or last baby, has a last.
As you take a moment to breathe,
you are faced with the realisation that in the intensity
of the season your motherhood has already changed.
It feels like you have said "hello" and "goodbye"
to multiple versions of your children without getting
the chance to get to know them all completely.
And like a punch to the gut, it hurts.
But in time, which you do get back,
you see the bigger picture.
You see them together, and thriving
and cheering each other on.
You see them filling the gaps with moments
you couldn't give them on your own
even if you had the time.
And above all else you realise that not every second
of every day needs to be a memory of you.
It can in fact be a memory of feeling loved by you,
and those special others who share your heart too.

CHAPTER SIX

PHYSICAL LOAD

*The load is heavy because you have children to love
and a family that means everything,
not because you are weak.*

Chapter Six

Slowing

It's the rushing when my children don't need me,
and trying to slow down when they do,
that underpins so much of the motherhood experience
in my opinion.
When I get a moment, I'm rushing like my day
depends on it, because it does. Kind of.
I get everything sorted in the morning for their entire
day in the brief moments of them playing.
I rush because I never know how long I'll have.
I catch up on the morning's dishes when my baby sleeps
and the others have quiet time.
I try to stop and rest too, but if I do, I get behind
and that makes it so much more work
when I don't have the energy.
And I rush because there's so much to do
in too short a window.
I reset the house and catch up on work with my husband
after they are all in bed.
And I rush because more than anything I want some time
left over for myself before I fall asleep, or someone wakes.
And that's always a lottery.

But when they do need me,
I slow down and be there for them.
Almost all the time anyway.
Sometimes other things just can't wait,
and the rush speeds up momentarily so I can be there
for them faster –
This is life.
So I sit with them. I hold them.
I leave things on hold and help them.
Because they are more important than any rush.
But this is how it goes, when viewing the bigger picture.
It's rushing to slowing in the matter of a few minutes,
if not seconds.
It's stopping then starting.
It's a rush of adrenaline, then catching my breath.
My body feels so weak.
And I used to think it was,
as I picked apart my tired frame in the mirror.
But it's strong.
It's agile.
Fast, slow, fast, slow, I repeat every day.
This body and mind that's shifting on demand is a temple,
even if it feels like the foundations are crumbling
some days.
"This body and mind can get me through anything",
I tell it, as I rush past the mirror, and I slow for my kids.

CHAPTER SIX

Love language

There are a million little ways I love you every single day.

It's waking up and carrying you to the kitchen.
Making you breakfast.
And then cuddling you before you get changed.

It's finding your drink bottle.
Applying your sunblock.
And then packing the extra pair of clothes just in case.

It's packing your lunch.
Making sure you brush your teeth.
And then driving you where you need to go.

It's preparing your dinner.
Organising your appointments.
And then washing your clothes in time for that special event.

Everlasting Motherhood

It's helping you in the bath.
Hearing about your day.
And then making sure your night light is charged.

It's organising for tomorrow.
Reading the latest newsletter.
And then confirming the time for the play date.

This is my love language to you.
Because although I say, "I love you",
it's in these million little ways,
every single day, that I say it too.

Chapter Six

Does it really matter?

Does it really matter that the house is a mess?
That you are a few minutes late?
Or that the plates aren't colour coordinated?

Does it really matter that the television was on a little
too much today?
That there were no greens on the plate?
Or that bedtime was later tonight?

Does it really matter that you are wearing the same thing
as yesterday?
That your children don't want to wear the warm jersey?
Or that you have to postpone the play date?

When you are in the thick of early motherhood,
it can feel like these things really do matter.

But when you pause and take a deep breath,
when you consider the whole scheme of things
(in life and your motherhood)
these things don't really matter, do they?

Showing up for them does.
Loving them does.
Being their person through it all does.

When they are little –
all that really matters to them is you.

Reframe

What if instead of thinking –
"If I don't get to the washing, the dishes,
or the house today, I'll be behind for the week",

we thought –
"If I don't get to the cuddles, the play
or the quality time with them while it's right in front of me,
I'll be behind for the rest of my life"?

Because that, for me, puts it all into perspective.

Chapter Six

Selfish

My children won't remember a lot of the early years.
I know that.
But the little things I do for them every day,
the moments that I make happen –
These will be part of who they become one day.
So they benefit eventually.
But everything else that I add to their life during this time,
that they may not benefit from through memory,
or their physical and emotional make up –
I will enjoy myself.
I will take all the moments that I have poured
my heart and soul into,
and rewatch them like my favourite shows.
Because I have given so much to these years.
And for once in my motherhood,
just once,
I am allowed to be selfish.

Unfinished business

You won't notice it at first –
But eventually you will make dinner in one go.
You will wash the clothes, fold the clothes
and put the clothes away in one day.
You will get to sorting the drawers stuffed with
random things, and the bags of odd socks,
maybe even more than once in a blue moon.
Eventually the things that used to feel impossible
or overwhelming or too hard to start, won't anymore.
You will find the energy and have the time to do them.
You will see that all that worrying
about what you haven't done in the past
really was for nothing.
And then you will sit with all the finished,
and feel a new type of unfinished business.
Because you won't notice it at first –
But your children really did grow up.

CHAPTER SEVEN

MENTAL LOAD

*The biggest thing about the mental load isn't the size.
It's the pressure not to forget.
Because we don't want to let our children down,
so we keep trying to remember more,
even if it means letting ourselves down in the process.*

'Mum will know'

I know…
I know the time it starts.
Where it takes place.
Who needs to be where.
I know how many lunches are needed.
Why they need their towels.
When they are expected to be finished.
I know where the socks were left.
Who needs a form.
When the order needs to go in by.
Right now, I know every little detail.
About everything.
For them.
"Mum will know", they say,
without a doubt in their minds.
And they're right.
While they can't, I will.
Because knowing everything they need is my thing.

CHAPTER SEVEN

Overstimulated

Sometimes I think I'm overstimulated because of the noise,
the fighting, the mess, the brightly coloured toys,
or being lucky enough to be in this sort of
constant human contact.
And much of this is valid.
But maybe the root cause of my overstimulation
is what's inside of me.
The invisible load of motherhood in my head
that encompasses so much more than what I see and hear.
The lists. The remembering. The details.
The invisible feelings that contaminate my mind
more than I care to admit.
The guilt. The shame. The gaslighting.
The invisible thoughts that move through my entire body.
The worrying. The questioning. The doubt.
This is the soundtrack that doesn't stop,
or even slow some days.
And even so, I don't know it off by heart.
I think I get overstimulated because I care so much
and love so deeply from the inside, not because I can't handle
the too-muchness of everything around me
and on the outside.
And it's easier when I treat it as such.

Everything else

More than anything I want my children to see the fun,
energetic, and relaxed version of me.
And I know that part of me is still there.
But sometimes I struggle to find it.
So, they see the ordinary, tired,
and often overwhelmed version of me instead.
I hope they know I'm more than this version.
Because I am.
And I hope they know it's not because of them
that they sometimes get this version either.
Because it's not.
It's everything else.

CHAPTER SEVEN

Break

When I say "I need a break" what I really mean is…
"I need a break from the dishes. The laundry.
And the meal prep / I need a break from the schedules.
The appointments. And all those constant mental notes
/ I need a break from the missed calls about something
important. The guilt for something I couldn't fit in.
And the self-shame over something I did my best at / I
need a break from being everywhere while also doing
all the little things while also regulating my emotions,
my hormones and my tired".
When I say "I need a break" what I really mean is…
"I need a break from the physical and mental load,
not from my kids".

Alone

It's Friday night.
The children are asleep.
My husband is out.
And the house is as clean as it will ever be these days.
It's quiet.
Calm.
And I'm the closest I have been to feeling relaxed
for a while.
I sink into this moment.
Just me, myself and I.
Because even though sometimes I feel lonely
when with my favourite people
throughout the days and nights,
for a little while, some days,
at the end of a long day –
I just need to be alone.

Chapter Seven

Queen

The forms are filled out.
The appointments are booked.
And the toilet rolls are replaced.

The clothes are washed.
The meals are prepared.
And the big emotions embraced.

Yet your diary's outdated.
Your clothes are the same.
And your meals have been had in a rush.

Your feelings are delayed.
Your appointments are overdue.
And your sleep is never enough.

It's easy to feel invisible –
Like your work
remains unseen.

But really you are invincible –
Mothering,
like a Queen.

CHAPTER EIGHT

TIME IN IMPORTANT WORK
(Working inside and outside of the home)

*Stay-at-home mothers (SAHM's) don't just stay at home.
Working mothers don't just work outside of the home.
All mothers mother first.
And how they do that is entirely their own business.*

Chapter Eight

What a SAHM needs

You come home on your lunch break to find your wife
holding back the tears as she tries to explain to you
how hard the morning has been.
Her words are not coming out right.
And even if you do not know exactly what to say,
you know what not to say.
You don't tell her how tired you are.
You don't turn your efforts into a competition.
You don't look around the house, see the mess
and comment on it.
What you do is embrace her
while the children are watching.
You hold onto her tight and let her say
whatever she still needs to say.
You tell her you are proud of her
and that she is doing a great job.
Because you may not always have the right words,
but you mean what you say.
Because you know that loving her right
is loving your entire family.
Because although she deserves the ends of the earth,
on a particularly hard day,
like today,
you know that's all she really needs.

SAHM salary

My husband got paid today.
I looked in our account, and there it was.
Recognition for all his hard work.
The long hours on the job.
The price he is paid for getting it done.
He deserves it, and we need it.
Boy, I'm thankful.
But I don't get the same for my job as a SAHM.
I work so hard every day, and night.
I literally have never worked harder.
Yet mine is purely a labour of love.
My money invisible, like so much of my work.
But that work – that all-consuming, exhausting,
relentless work that comes with being a full time mother –
it comes with a wage. Just not the usual type.

Chapter Eight

Right now my wage is in the slower mornings
I get to have with my kids.
It's in the cuddles we have throughout the day.
It's in the new firsts I get to see,
and the lasts I may never see again.
I get paid through the quiet little moments we share
when no one else is watching,
and the chaotic days filled with so much joy.
And boy am I lucky.
No one hands me a check for being a SAHM.
But my kids hand me the lottery.
Because I may be broke financially,
but I am rich in heart and soul.

Time in

After you have a baby time off work
is time in important work.
Maybe you get paid, maybe you don't.
All that matters now is that you are holding your life's work.
From this moment on, you want to give them
the best possible chance at living.
And this may look different for you than for your friends.
You will do it the way you need to, within your own means,
within your own morals,
with or without support of your own.
And even if you return to work eventually, fully,
or in some capacity, you know, just like the next mother
who may be doing her work slightly differently to yours,
that motherhood always comes first.
Even if you live and breathe your work outside of the home,
your heart is always in the work of loving your children
the best you can.

Chapter Eight

Maternity leave is not just the time you have at home
after you have a baby.
It is every single day afterwards too.
Because you are never really the same.
Your priorities shift.
The day that you have your baby,
you leave your work outside of the home as one person,
and if you return to work you bring someone
entirely different.
As someone who has skills that they never had to have
before, with a reason to show up like they never have before,
but with their heart forever in motherhood first.
That's why we are mistaken.
It's not "maternity leave".
Its eternity leave.

Bonus

I used to think having it all was having a family and a career.
But now that I have a family,
now that I have children who are healthy,
who wake up in our family home,
who fill up every single space of our time,
who smile, laugh, and cry
because they are here, with us, as part of our life,
now that I have a husband who loves me,
supports me and appreciates me through it all –
I think I already have it all.
Everything else is just a bonus.

Chapter Eight

String to her bow

She's lived a thousand lives before this one.
Did you know?
You see her in her current season.
Children live off her as she moves,
a new identity, finding more of her every day.
And maybe she does look tired.
Or like she needs a new wardrobe.
That's not news to her.
But this isn't all there is to her,
even though they are her everything.
There are more strings to her bow.
And maybe one day she will explore them again,
or try to add more,
but as a mother first this time.
She will be even better than before because of it.
Don't you think?
Or did you forget that motherhood
is a string to her bow too?

Workforce application letter

To whom it may concern,

I wish to apply for your position in the workforce. Below is what I can offer BECAUSE of motherhood:

Intensive multi-tasking skills. I can do so many things at once. My mind is everywhere, but all over what needs to happen in the now. I have a triage system that helps me juggle many balls at once. You can trust it. I do. And so do my children.

I am hyper-aware of my areas needing work. I am constantly trying to better these areas. I strive to be the best for my children and myself. Nothing has been more of a catalyst for self-development than motherhood, and this flows into every other aspect of my life.

I am more creative. I think outside of the box because I have to. I may have less time, but thinking on the spot is second nature now.

Chapter Eight

I may be late sometimes and ask for leniency, but you should see my work ethic. I know what "hard work" really is now. I have never had to dig so deep in my life. And so, I've found a deeper strength and resilience in my ability to work.

I am asked to remain calm under pressure daily.
Hardly anything phases me anymore. And when it does, my focus is adapting to it. I am dependable when things turn to custard, which I now also know is inevitable some days.

My family will always come first. But my family is also my reason for showing up every day in whatever capacity is required "of me", "for us". I will never let you down, even if it means never letting them down.

Thank you for your time and consideration.
I'm grateful to motherhood for mine.

CHAPTER NINE

DAY IN MY LIFE

I may have lost my spark for now,
but everything my children touch turns to gold.
So, I am rich, even when depleted.
I am living in an abundance of purpose,
even when I don't recognise myself.
They glisten and so do I.

Chapter Nine

Master of one

Being a Mother is feeling like you're the Jack of all Trades
and the Master of None.
You need to be in so many places at once,
often feeling behind in it all.
You are always doing multiple things at once,
often feeling like you cannot give enough to each.
You feel like the Master of showing up with everything
you have,
and to everything that is required of you by your family,
just like that superhero who always saves the day.
But underneath all that effort,
all that showing up,
all that here, there and everywhere –
is someone feeling spread so thin.
Someone feeling they can do everything to survive
but nothing to thrive.
A Master of None.
But who said that what you feel is a true reflection
of who you are?
Who said that you can't be the Jack of all Trades
and the Master of One?
Because I know one thing you master every single day.
And that's loving your kids,
in your own special way.

High-functioning

I used to call myself productive.
Now I think I'm more high-functioning.
Because motherhood has made me even more
productive in different ways,
but without breaks or enough sleep in between.
So comparatively speaking I function at a high level constantly
by doing the things my family needs of me
even when I feel at a low level.
I am a high-functioning mother.
When in the thick of it –
We all are.

Chapter Nine

Always something

When raising little children there's always something.
Someone's sick.
Someone's having a hard day.
Someone's wanting something they can't have.
And if it's not that, then something has been forgotten.
Something is not working.
Something just isn't helping your tired.
Every day you know there will be at least something
challenging you have to face.
Something you have to overcome.
Something until the next thing
without a break between anything.
But there's something about being someone's
"all they could ever wish for" isn't there?
There's something about knowing
you can show up through everything, right?
There's something about being a mum
that makes this such a skill,
not a burden,
don't you think?
"Always something"
always means something
when family means everything.

nervous system

I'm not being chased by a bear.
It's just my toddler having a meltdown.
I'm being rushed to help someone who's stubbed their toe.
And then there's the milk that's spilled
all over the kitchen floor.

I'm not trapped in a cage with hungry lions.
It's just that my children might be late for school.
The baby won't stop crying in the car.
And I realise I've forgotten to pack the nappies
and a spare change of clothes
right when someone needs those things.

I'm not trying to swim away from a shark.
My children are just fighting sleep.
I halved a banana so they could share.
And the dishwasher is beeping,
the washing machine needs emptying
and the boxes of Lego have been tipped out
all over the hallway.

I'm not in danger.
But sometimes it feels like it.
I'm safe.
I'm okay.
Everything is under control.
I just need my nervous system to believe it.

Chapter Nine

Alone time

Sometimes I have time away from them.
I love the time to myself,
but I hate not being there for them.
I know it's healthy to have breaks, but it doesn't feel like it.
I sit to relax, get into a good book
or more than one episode of a show – FINALLY…
But my mind is still with them.
I wonder what they are doing, how they are doing
and so I almost don't do anything I said I'd do
with this time.
Why am I doing this to myself?
I'm away from them like my body has needed,
but I don't really want to be.
I'm there, but not.
It's confusing.
A push/pull of want and need.
I need this, but I want them –
Even though I know I can't always have both.
Being with them almost all the time is beautifully
exhausting, relentless and all-consuming.
It's also the one place I love to be.
They want me to come home.
I know that.
And truthfully,
they're not the only ones.

More to lose

I feel this pit in my stomach when doing certain things now.
Things that aren't even necessarily dangerous.
Just everyday things that I didn't used to think twice about.
Like driving after a heavy frost.
Or flying to get to a holiday destination.
Like entering a busy mall I've never been to before.
Or standing on a high bridge.
It doesn't matter if my children are with me or not.
Although it's worse then.
My mind thinks of so many "what ifs"
and worst case scenarios.
I didn't think my mind would ever have such control
over me.
But it does now.
My heart runs my mind.
Because having children means –
There's so much more to lose.

CHAPTER NINE

My life

I went to the door.
I saw my kids playing outside with my husband.
I watched them for a minute or two.
It was the most beautiful frame of the day.
I called out "dinners ready" and watched them
as they ran to me with smiles from ear to ear,
just like they do in the movies.
It was the happy ending we all wait for.
Except this isn't a movie.
This is my life.
And I get to live it every single day.

One more day

If you told me I had just one more day at the stage of life
I am currently in, I wouldn't say I want to bungee jump,
or swim with the dolphins.

I would say I want to hold their little hands in mine
for as long as possible and feel what it is to let them
be the first to let go of every cuddle.

I would say I want to lie with them during every nap,
and wait for them to wake in my arms, to have one
more chance at seeing their eyes be the first to meet mine.

I would say I want to watch as they turn our house into
their very own playground. Their happy place would be
mine and the aftermath would be something to behold,
not begrudge. I'd want to be in it forever.

CHAPTER NINE

I would say I want to hear them call "Mama" as many times as possible, and tell them I love them in every which way. These are the words that will always mean the most.

I would say I want to do the ordinary things.
The everyday things. The things that on any other day would feel like the same-old things. Because these things are the big things. The life-changing things. The things that I know are the best because they are there with me.

I would then say one day isn't nearly enough time,
but they are worth more than every second of mine.
And so, I'd take every moment and be in it,
because this is where, out of everywhere, I'd choose to be.

CHAPTER TEN

SPECIAL OCCASION

Every year there are holidays and celebrations at certain times of the year. A mother works hard behind the scenes during these periods. But for her, they are not a break. In fact, they often leave her more exhausted than beforehand. She does it because she has a childhood in her hands, and she knows that memories matter.

Chapter Ten

Currency

A mother will spend hours wrapping presents
for them to be ripped open in mere seconds.
She will stay up late at night blowing up balloons
for them to be popped before the party.
She will use every last ounce of energy she has
to move the Elf late at night
all for him to be found before she can say
"Good morning".
Because seeing the joy in her children's eyes
(even if only for a moment)
is all she ever wants.
That's her currency.

Wish list

Want:
my children.

Need:
my husband.

Wear:
little arms around my neck,
growing bodies on my hips
and familiar hands within mine.

Read:
every little detail of them today
like it's already yesterday.

And as I hear "mum" from the other room
while holding a baby on my chest,
or watching my husband play games with them,
while I watch them all existing
on a random Sunday morning –
I'm grateful,
as always,
that Christmas came early this year.

Chapter Ten

Magic master

Everyone else sees the magic as the children
open their presents.
I see the mother having spent weeks organising them
and then hours late at night wrapping them.

Everyone else sees the excited children
playing with their family members.
I see the mother holding her overstimulated
and overtired babies when everyone else goes home.

Everyone else sees the perfect family photos
and the happy family posts.
I see the mother who has given everything to keep it all
on track, even when she's felt like she's going off the rails.

I see you magic master and memory maker.
You are responsible for the bigger picture.
And it's beautiful.

Credit

When they ask –
"Who got you through your motherhood this year?"
You may say your husband.
You may say your children.
You may say your friends,
your sister,
your own mother.
You may say a lot of things,
and give credit to a lot of different people.
You also may not.
But please don't forget the one person
who truly got you through.
The one who has been there before everyone else,
and always has.
Please,
please,
whatever you do,
don't forget about you.

Chapter Ten

Mother's Day

This Mother's Day I want you to know
that you are worth more than one day.
So much more than one day.
You are someone's every day.
Someone's constant.
Someone's unwavering support.
You're behind the scenes.
You're a cheerleader.
You're on the sidelines.
You're absolutely everywhere they need you to be.
And it doesn't stop.
It never stops.
Not for one day.
Not for two days.
Not ever.
Even when those children have outgrown your home.
Even when those children have their own children.
This Mother's Day I hope you know how cherished you are.
I hope you know how valued you are.
I hope you know how seen you are.
This Mother's Day I hope you know how strong you are.
I hope you know how much you are giving.
I hope you know that you are an amazing Mum.
But above all,
This Mother's Day
I hope you know you deserve so much more than one day.

Motherhood occasion

Turn the music up and dance together in the kitchen.
Blow bubbles while they bounce on the trampoline.
Dress the cake with sprinkles
and cut the sandwiches into fun little shapes.
Have picnics in the living room.
Make forts on a random weeknight.
Bring out the antique toys
that have been through generations.
Put your face on and style your hair for a day at home.
Take yourself out and buy something nice.
Make a sweet treat after they have gone to bed.
Don't wait.
Do these things every day.
Because the special occasion is motherhood.

CHAPTER ELEVEN

STRUGGLING

*Maybe you're not meant to find this easy.
Maybe if you're doing your best to get it right,
parenting will be one of the hardest things
you will ever do.*

Groundhog Day

When you have been in the thick of mothering
for a long time you realise so much of it
is trying to find the magic in the mundane again.
Because while so much of it is right in front of you,
it is the most beautiful thing you will ever get to see
on a daily basis –
the groundhog nature of much of it day after day
takes a toll on you.
So much so,
that you have to make a conscious effort to be mindful.
That's the unspoken truth.
And making sense of it isn't easy.

CHAPTER ELEVEN

Contradictions

Advice mothers are given, in no particular order…

Don't lose yourself. Have something for yourself.
It's so important. But also immerse yourself in it.
Enjoy every moment. Blink and you'll miss it.

Work. Even if you don't need to. Teach your children
it's important. But don't put your children into day care.
You didn't have children to have others care for them.
Find your village.

Stay home if you can. They are only so small for so long.
Surely your career can wait. But you need to keep them
socialised, the home in order, oh, and take care of
yourself too. We managed. You are so blessed.

Eat well. Exercise often. Do what fills your cup.
Self-care isn't selfish. But also, your children should
come first. They should be your priority. They need
you most right now.

Look after your relationship. Make time for it.
Your partner needs you too. But first and foremost,
make sure you fit in family time. And that your partner
has one-on-one time with your children too.

Don't give your children too much screen time.
Processed food isn't good for them. Don't use a
pacifier. But survive. Do what you need to.
These are some of the hardest years of your life.

Cuddle your babies. They won't always be in your bed.
Enjoy it. But encourage their independence. Don't make a
rod for your own back. You are in charge.

You are doing such a good job. It's difficult. Keep going.
But don't complain too much, you sound ungrateful.

Mothers everywhere…
This is hard enough as it is.

Chapter Eleven

What I really mean

When I say "This is hard",
I am not complaining about my children.
"This" is not "them".

"This" is guilt perpetuated by the constant
information overload about what we "should" be doing
with our children, or how we "should" be doing it.

"This" is the state of the world we are parenting in
and the constant gratitude wrapped in worry.

"This" is society, and what seems to be a move away
from a parent's worth in the home,
particularly in the early years.

"This" is the expectation placed on women
to work like they don't have children
and to have children like they don't work.

"This" is the mental load that never takes a break
and the physical load that, in modern times,
is enough to break you.

"This" is unpacking your entire life before having children,
as you work out how you want to live your life with them.

"This" is managing. Time. Finances.
Physical and mental health. Family. Friends.
Social interaction. Work. Life. Everything in between.

"This" is the tired that comes from the above alone.
And then the tired that comes from not sleeping too.

"This" is not them.
It never has been.
"This" is everything else.

"Complaining" about "This" has nothing to do with
how much I love my children (although if you must
know the "how much" is astronomical).
But it does have everything to do with
how human I am (how human we ALL are).

CHAPTER ELEVEN

Signs

If I was struggling, I probably wouldn't tell you.
But there would be signs.
I'd say, "I'm fine thanks" and smile when you see me.
My children would be turning up to things as per usual.
And I'd be showing up too.
I'd be organising things for my family, and telling you
"I have everything under control" when you offer to help.
I may look semi put together or be wearing a new outfit.
My house may even look tidier than the last time you visited.
See?
A reminder that the signs for mothers who may be struggling may not be obvious.
Be there anyway.

Differences

My clean is someone's dirty.
My hard is someone's easy.
My village is someone's nothing.
My health is someone's goal.
My home is someone's house.
My family is someone's dream.

We don't all have the same motherhood.
But we can all take a moment to appreciate what we have,
and a long deep breath after acknowledging what we don't.

Chapter Eleven

Ups and downs

I'm in motherhood –
I'm okay,
until I'm not.
I'm better than ever,
until I'm not.
I'm my best version of me,
until I'm not.
I'm in motherhood –
where the highs from love are so very high,
and the lows from exhaustion are so very real.
I'm in motherhood –
where the highs last,
and last,
and last,
until the exhaustion won't allow any more of it,
and then I crack under the weight of it all
in a mere few seconds.
I'm in motherhood –
and I've never been so up and down,
while consistently showing up.

Masking

I'm overstimulated ("Mum's trying")
I'm exhausted ("Mum's a little tired")
I'm hangry ("Mum's coming")
I'm overwhelmed ("Mum's okay")
I'm hormonal ("Mum's got you")
I'm worried ("Mum's here")

I'm going through a lot of things because –
"motherhood".
Yet I try my best to hand them the softer version because –
"childhood".
And I'm proud of me for that.

CHAPTER ELEVEN

Same same

When your babies are having a hard time,
they tell you to put them in water or take them outside.
But as a mother to those babies,
who is allowed to have hard times too –
have you ever put yourself in water or taken yourself outside
when things feel a lot?
Because I think you'll find the same principles apply,
and it works.

What you are

You're not broken.
You're tired.

You're not boring.
You're busy.

You're not invisible.
You're always there.

You're a mother,
not a superhuman.

And it feels hard,
because it is.

Chapter Eleven

Breathe

I'm still at the –
can't finish anything, forget the day,
am late a lot, stay up longer than I should,
have broken sleep, complain I'm tired,
have a messy home, don't drink enough water,
accidentally miss meals, live off coffee,
enjoy silence, have stained clothes,
weird hair styles, and no spare time stage.

But my babies are still at the stage
where they need me more than I need me.
So, I keep rallying,
living off the glimmers within.

Because it's not forever.
It's not forever.
Breathe, it's not forever.

But also –
grab the tissues,
because it's not forever.

Eventually

The first baby introduces you to motherhood
and every new stage that lays ahead of you.
The last baby asks you to leave behind
every version of motherhood you have come to know.
You cannot be prepared for either.
But you can know that you will be okay eventually.
Your children need you to be.

CHAPTER TWELVE

FRIENDSHIPS

*May we always remember what it takes
to be the friend we needed while in early motherhood.*

What's it like?

I sit with my friend who is 8 months pregnant
and she asks me what it's like.
My mind immediately goes to the things
that are the hardest for me right now.
You will be to-the-bone exhausted.
You will have little time to yourself.
Your relationship with your husband will change.
You will find parts of yourself that you never knew existed.
But in doing so you will find parts of yourself
you will need to work really hard on.
You will feel guilty a lot of the time.
You will feel like you are not enough a lot of the time.
You won't see your friends as much.
You will likely lose some of your passions along the way.

But I don't tell her that,
because I know she will figure that out in her own time.
Because when you are a soon-to-be mum,
largely what you need is optimism.
Because there's no going back.
This is going to be her life.

So, my mind takes me to these parts –
You will feel a love like you've never experienced before.
You will find such strength within yourself.
Your relationship will face its challenges,
but you can become stronger through them.

Chapter Twelve

There is nothing like seeing your husband become a dad.
It can be one of the most beautiful parts of this process.
You will find out who your true friends are.
And that can be a real blessing.
You will find such purpose in what you are doing.
The way you view the world will be slightly different.
You'll be softer now.
You'll be more vulnerable.
And that doesn't need to be seen as a negative.
It can be your greatest power.
You'll say you would die for them,
but there's even more reason to live for them.
And for a snippet of time you will be someone's everything.
You will be there for everything,
and they will come to you for everything.
It is so life-changing, in the best way.
Nothing really compares to becoming a mum
for the first time.

And so I tell her that.
I tell her "you are about to embark
on the most amazing journey of your life
and I'm so excited for you".
Because that's the truth too.
And when she's in it, like me,
we can talk about the other parts.
Because when you are in it,
largely what you need is validation.

Next time

You have a mum friend who knows all the right things
to say.
You meet for coffee and this is how the conversation goes…

"What have you been up to?" she asks.
"Just the same old things," you tell her with a shrug.
"Nothing overly exciting unfortunately."
"Excuse me?" she responds quickly.
"I want to hear every little detail
about what you have been up to recently.
Your ordinary is extraordinary.
Your life is exciting and purposeful
and what you are doing is important."
"Oh, I just thought…" you start.
"Please tell me," she politely interrupts.
"I've been looking forward to hearing about this all week."

And she keeps her attention as you tell her about the
socks that were left at the stadium, the dropped naps,
the new words of the week, some recent favourite toys,
the school calendar, how you put the dishwashing powder
in the fridge and the butter in the washing machine,
what you haven't had a chance to get done all week
and what was had for breakfast on Tuesday morning.

Chapter Twelve

"Thank you for sharing that with me," she says.
"It's nice to know I'm not the only one."
You laugh together, have more coffee and then she tells you
about her daily mad-morning rush,
the new dress she bought for her daughter,
what happened at pick-up on Wednesday,
how her toddler ripped up her meeting notes,
why she couldn't stop laughing when her son woke up
from a nap, what meals no one is eating,
her favourite book at the moment, and how she removed
the scribbles of permanent marker from the coffee table.

"It sounds like you have been busy," you tell her.
"I have," she says. "You know what that's like."

And after some more coffee, cake and stories of solidarity you
both decide to part ways.
"See you next time," she says as she walks out the door.
And you know you will.
Because for this sort of friend,
there's always a next time.

More than me

You visit me when I'm ready.
You've done this before, but it's different this time.
I offer you a cuddle with my new baby.
We both know it's my last.
I see your eyes start to well as you notice every little detail.
You are realising that you don't have this anymore.
I don't have much longer of having this anymore either –
A truth hitting close to home for me.
We don't talk about that though.
Neither of us are ready yet.
You tell me how beautiful he is.
And I tell you how grateful I am
that you're here to meet him.
I tell you about the birth,
and postpartum life this time around.
And you tell me about what's going on
in your busy family life.
You hand him back to me, ever so gently.
"Thank you for the cuddle," you say.
You insist that you put the dishes away,
fold some clothes that are on the kitchen table,
and stack my toddler's blocks away.

Chapter Twelve

I thank you for your help.
Before you leave you lean over my baby tenderly
and embrace us both for longer than usual.
You look into my eyes.
"I'm here for you," is all you say.
But your eyes tell me more.
They say, "I miss my babies as babies.
I wish I could turn back time.
I would give anything to have one more cuddle
with the younger versions of my children.
Enjoy every minute.
Every second.
Every breath.
It goes by too fast".
On your way out you tell me not to get up
and that you've put the meal you brought around
in the fridge.
But I get up.
I insist.
And I hug you tight.
Because I know you need it today.
Perhaps even more than me.

That friend

You're that friend.
The one who drops things at the door postpartum,
and texts me later to say, "I hope you are doing okay".
The one who keeps wanting to visit when my babies
are no longer newborns and everyone else
has quietened down.
The one who comes around so we can share in our
mess (not just the mess we can see).
You're that friend who doesn't take it personally
when I don't message back for a long time,
and keeps sending me funny videos anyway.
The one who my kids treat as an aunty
even though we are not related.
And the one who helps me because you want to,
despite having so much going on yourself.
You're that friend.
The one of few friends.
The very special friend that every mum needs
but not every mum gets.
And I just hope you know –
I'm trying to be that friend to you too.

CHAPTER THIRTEEN

MARRIAGE

*Motherhood and fatherhood will never be the same.
No matter how much is fair, shared and equal,
in love and in labour,
the experiences of one will always be different from the other's.
Remember that, with grace.
It's biology.*

Dad

"A man's life doesn't really change when he becomes a father…"
Really?
Because I know it's not the same as being a mother.
The two cannot be compared.
But change is needed.
The mother of his growing child needs him during pregnancy.
To do so, he needs to say "no" to other things more
and say "yes" to her mostly.
She needs him early postpartum.
She's an entirely different person now
and he needs to meet her again with arms wide open
regardless of what he thought life would or could look like
at this point.
And as she finds her groove in motherhood,
he should continue to be there for her and their children
as they grow, evolve, and change.
And he should change with them,
accommodating their needs when he can.
A man's life may not change as much as a mother's does
after parenthood.
But it should change.
And if it really does,
that's what makes him more than a father.
That's what makes him a dad.

Chapter Thirteen

Wearing motherhood

"How was your day?" you ask me.

Sometimes I tell you, "It's been hard. I've not done enough. We were late to this and that and everything. The washing still isn't done. I didn't get a chance to shower after you left. The dog didn't stop barking. And I've been grumpy, so I feel bad about that".

Sometimes I just say "good", because I can't string another single thought or sentence together.

And sometimes I tell you, "We've actually had a great day today", because in the last hour or so things have been easier and enjoyable and as perfect as life could ever be even though it didn't always feel that way.

My days are largely the same, but how I experience them are slightly different. So, after a long day of your own, you don't know what you are coming into every night. There is no real predictability to me for now, other than being "pretty tired" and "very in love with our little family".

Everlasting Motherhood

I wear motherhood like this. For better and for worse.
An ever-changing outfit, not always fit for every
season, but clothed, nonetheless.

And I don't know if it will always be like this,
but thank you for loving me in every outfit
and through every season.
You are keeping me steady on this runway –
every trip, wobble and wardrobe malfunction
along the way.

I know how lucky I am.
And those little footsteps walking in our shadows
will someday too.

Chapter Thirteen

Roommates

Sometimes it feels like we're roommates.
Two people who met in the house they find themselves in
and go about their days in parallel.
We eat breakfast when we each need to –
hardly together.
And then we meet again at the end of the day –
small conversations are exchanged because we are that tired.
The toothbrushes are in the same place.
So are our shoes, and cars.
And we share a bedroom together,
although there's often more room between us
than time in bed,
as we are needed by others then.
But we didn't meet this way.
Or live the life we sometimes describe it as.
We met and fell in love.
We decided to create a family.
And now we have these beautiful children together.
We live in this home.

Everlasting Motherhood

With them at our feet, and their love all around us.
We have moments of connection in times shared with them.
And those moments – no matter how big or small –
make us feel more in love than ever.
This is a stage in our romantic tale,
not a contract between acquaintances.
And sure, this life comes with challenges.
But nothing good has ever came easy,
especially not in a season as life-changing and meaningful
as this one.
This is where we are, for this tiny part of their lives
and for this small chapter in our marriage
where they need us more than anyone else.
So we adapt, show compassion,
and let things look different for a while.
And then we remember where they came from.
Two soulmates.
Not roommates.
Two hearts and souls brought together,
with those children the heart and soul of us.
Not just now,
but forever.

Chapter Thirteen

Hand in hand

With each child, there's been more room between us
and less chance to bridge the gap.
What started as the touching of hips as we sat on the
couch, has overtime turned into not being able to
reach each other at all.
We glance over their tiny heads, and try to get a
word in, but we end up saying "we'll try again later".
Then later comes and we have either forgotten what
we were trying to talk about,
or we are both too tired to talk about much anyway.
So we leave it for another day.
And thankfully we both know that day will come.
We both understand that the current stage we are in
is only a fraction of our parenthood journey.
That's something we do manage to talk about at least.
It's not our time, and it is.
It's the time of our lives with the family
we created from what started as just us.
And when the "just us" stage comes again
we may not know where to start,
but we will hopefully have all the time in the world
again to figure it out.
Hopefully we will have all the memories of good days,
hard days and days of getting through it all together
to raise our beautiful young family,
to remind us that we can do it –
Hand in hand this time.

needs

If you asked me what I need most in my motherhood journey right now –
I wouldn't say sleep or time for me.
I wouldn't say a cleaner or frozen meals.
I wouldn't even say a village of support
for every aspect of my mothering.
(Although these things would never go unappreciated.)
I just need you,
loving me in my harsher moments,
and supporting me in my fragile ones.
Quietly lifting heavy when I can't,
and cheering me on when I can.
Being there first when I feel like I'm coming last,
and lasting through everything.
You're the behind the scenes in my motherhood.
I need you more than anyone or anything right now.
And thankfully, you're here.

Chapter Thirteen

Team

I work hard.
You work hard.

I'm tired.
You're tired.

Everything I do is for them.
Everything you do is for them.

We are in this together.
A team.
Just in different roles.
And with varying capacities.

It's not a competition.
It's not a competition.
It's not a competition.

Here's to us remembering that.

Best day(s) of my life

The day I got married was a great day.
But it wasn't the best day of my life.
That day was when I was with the man I married
meeting each of our children.
Every time we exchanged in-the-moment-vows of pride
in a hospital room in front of this new precious life.
There were no three course meals,
suits and ties or first dances.
We shared a certain takeaway,
wore whatever we felt most comfortable in
and had first holds as we talked about the birth,
the name, and what our other children may think.
We sat there looking at them,
and then each other
and we knew this was it.
We took all that love,
and made something really special out of it –
our forever people.
And nothing could ever beat that.

Chapter Thirteen

Snip

We drive to the doctor
because today is the day,
our new baby chapter
is being taken away.

And I know that we're ready.
I feel that we're complete.
I just can't seem to shake
this sense of disbelief.

My mind takes me back
to memories that got us here.
Holding our first baby
was only yesterday I swear.

I think about the time
I found out I'd be a mum,
and the times that then followed
with breathtaking outcome.

I think about the moments
when I didn't know I could,
but holding our precious babies
always meant I would.

I think about the two of us
and how much we've grown,
as we faced it all together
through every unknown.

Everlasting Motherhood

I think about my body
and what it's been through,
all the strength it's mustered
doing what it had to do.

I'm thankful it's your turn
to do what's to be done.
My gratitude for your facing it
has already begun.

But I have so many feelings
for these earlier versions of us
who've grown our little family
into memories we can trust.

And I can't wait to start this –
the new chapter that awaits.
I know deep down it's exciting –
what's next is going to be great.

But let us take a moment
to sit in what has been.
The challenges we've lived,
woven into a dream.

Let's thank each other in fullness
for all that we have made,
and hold each other tightly
as we enter our new stage.

Chapter Thirteen

Dear Husband

I don't know how we got here sometimes.
Do you?
I watch them, these babies born from us,
as they live in the home we have created for them.
They smile with joy as they play in our presence,
and run to us with tear-stained cheeks
when things go wrong.
Everything about them is perfect, and this life we live is too,
even if it is always a little rough around the edges –
Don't you think?
I remember the times I wondered how today would look.
If we'd get here, and be able to have this at all.
But here we are.
In these days, of us, them, and this little life.
Do you see?
We did this.
You and I.
We are doing big things in this little life.
And I'm so proud of us.

CHAPTER FOURTEEN

GROWING PAINS

Children don't just "fit into your life".
They change your life.
And you spend much of your time trying to still fit into theirs.

Chapter Fourteen

I get it now (last baby edition)

I get it now.
I get why you got emotional as you held my new baby.
I get why you told me to try and enjoy every moment.
I get why you said you wish you could go back
to the early days of motherhood.
As I see a new baby younger than my last,
I get it.
I see it clearly now.
I feel what you did too.
You weren't trying to invalidate me.
You were simply trying to warn me

– It won't be just like this ever again.

They were right

I've been sitting staring at this bag I've just packed.
It took me so long to get to this point.
Not just the packing.
But the years leading up to it.

Inside the bag are more than little baby clothes.
There are moments late at night with each of my babies,
cuddling them and holding onto their smallness of today
for one last time.
There are moments of joy as I watch them
reach new milestones, and sadness as I realise
they don't fit what they used to yesterday.
There are moments of long days together
with certain stains on certain pieces that won't come out,
reminding me of what we did sometimes
when we were at this stage together,
and that I actually quite like those permanent marks now.
When I look at this bag I think of the last few years.
I think of how my body created the most amazing
little people to fit into these pieces.

Chapter Fourteen

I'm so proud of it for that.
I think of how many times I've felt pushed to my limit,
but kept going to get them into that bigger size.
It's nice to see it that way.
I think of how much love I have received
from being the mother to those I clothe,
wash for and keep warm.
There has been no bigger privilege.

My last baby no longer fits into the clothes within this bag.
And so I sit with more than the clothes
as I pack them away for someone else's precious baby.
I sit with my motherhood to date.
I re-explore what has been.
I hold on to what is no longer, for that little bit longer.

Because I realise, here in this moment –
They were right.
It does go too fast.

Finality

Everything is so final.
The last time you walk out of the hospital
with your new baby.
The last time that same baby uses the bassinette.
The last time you give away newborn hand-me-downs
that have seen every one of your babies grow inside of them.
It's the reminders that this is it, forever.
The first time you start your cycle again
knowing there will be no more two-week waits.
The first time you have a night away
knowing they are okay without you overnight now.
The first time you sort through your maternity clothing
knowing you will never get to wear
these worn-out pieces again.
Every last with your know-it's-your-last is all so final.
So black and white.
So real.
The chapter is closing,
and you are signing your early motherhood away,
without any more hovering over the "sign here" sticker.
There's no going back now.
You know that, even if you can't quite believe it yet.
So you put on a brave face
and brace yourself for middle motherhood.
Because you are ready for it.
And you have so much to look forward to,
even if you can't quite believe it yet.

CHAPTER FOURTEEN

Without warning

One day you'll carry them on your chest.
And the next on your hips.
Then on some random night a few years later,
you'll be asked to give them a piggyback ride to bed.
These are the milestones of a child,
and the growing pains of a parent.
And every part of it feels huge,
because it is.

Shadows

It's late.
And you are in your big kid bed.
Yet still, I find myself lying next to you.
You don't need me here anymore.
But I want to be here more than ever.
I cuddle into your body,
just like you used to cuddle into mine.
It's the same, but different.
As I try not to make any sudden movements
(just like old times),
but without any risk of you waking until the morning
(which is a stage I never saw coming),
I can't help but think about when you still needed me
throughout the night.
It was beautiful, really.
Part of me still wants to be needed by you.
The huge-all-consuming-mother's-love-of-mine part.
I think it always will.
Please let me be there from time to time,
even when you don't need me to be.
I won't make it obvious, I promise.
I'll be in the shadows,
happy to simply be there.

Chapter Fourteen

Five

You've had a few birthdays now.
But something about the number five feels huge.
Maybe it's because I can no longer hear
the pitter-patter of your little feet,
and instead the sound of the impending school bell
ringing in my ears.
Maybe it's because I can't carry you as easily as I once did,
but somehow your body looks so tiny in a school bag.
Maybe it's because I don't remember
the last time you needed me to rock you to sleep,
and now I can't stop thinking about how quickly
the last few years have really gone as I replay so many of
the best moments of my life.
You are a big kid now.
And I feel like the baby you once were in my arms
only a short while ago.

Everlasting Motherhood

I know that you will always be my baby,
but this next stage asks me to let go of my grip
that little bit more.
More than any other stage we have walked hand in
hand through.
And the uncertainty of everything waiting before us
is so much bigger than before.
Maybe that's why this birthday feels a little different
from the rest.
But maybe it feels huge because it is.
Maybe it's because this love we have isn't little.
Maybe it's because it's bigger than any huge
uncertainty I have.
And maybe today, of all days, I need to remember that.

CHAPTER FOURTEEN

Six

You are six years old.
You wake up more slowly now.
Your body needs the rest these days.
As you stretch in your bed and say "good morning"
to your favourite teddies, you can hear your mum
in the kitchen trying to make a coffee quietly.
She's not talking and there's no one asking her for things
so you know your siblings aren't up yet.
Excitement comes over you.
You quietly get out of bed and tip-toe down the hallway
to find her.
You don't want to wake the others.
This one on one time doesn't always happen,
so you want to take your opportunity.
You open the door to find her.
There she is making everyone breakfast.

You run to her hips (as you do now) and she cradles you from above, before lifting you up and saying
"see, you're not too big for me yet".
She offers you breakfast.
You sit and eat while she sips her coffee.
You chat about your sleep, your dreams,
and what you want to do today.
You have a giggle about the burnt toast,
and cuddle together as you listen to the song on the playlist you both like.
It's your favourite part of the day already.
Shortly after, your siblings run in and things become louder.
Your mum is split in different directions
and your day of sharing begins.
You love it, really.
But for those few moments it was nice to have her
on her own.
Just you and her.
Especially as a big six-year-old,
who has so much to share.

Chapter Fourteen

More than mum

It's not what it was,
I know that now.
It's taken a few years,
to see that, somehow.

As they grow, they need
many different things.
At first that pulls,
hard on heart strings.

That baby of yours,
doesn't fit on your chest.
Or maybe they don't,
still need you for rest.

The toddler clothes
are no longer "cool".
And your time at home
becomes play after school.

The days of knowing
exactly what they need,
becomes days of trial,
doubting and plead.

Everlasting Motherhood

They're finding their feet
in shoes that don't fit.
And you are too,
by witnessing it.

But they will upsize
and find more room
in new shoes and people
before too soon.

In friends and teachers,
coaches and mentors.
Others who see
their interests are cared for.

They'll find new things
that you can't give,
cos of time, or skill,
or your younger kids.

And they will thrive
just like before,
even though you'll want
to be doing more.

Chapter Fourteen

But you will stay
holding big space
for the times they need
their special place.

And one day you'll see.
You'll understand why –
They had to grow up,
and say goodbye

to the versions of them
you knew so well,
stories of a childhood
you'll always tell.

They need you there,
just not quite the same.
In the back, to the side
but still in the frame.

It'll happen.
It needs to.
You'll see who they become.
And you'll be proud
when they see
a world more than Mum.

Loving you today

I see you growing every day,
but I don't really notice it,
until someone who hasn't seen you every day does,
a Facebook memory flashes before me,
or the size of yesterday suddenly doesn't fit.
The shock is my reality.
I smile,
cry inside,
and proclaim: "It goes so fast".
I look at you,
my baby again,
that same child I've known since before anyone else,
and think –
"Watching you grow is the best experience of my life.
And even if it hurts a little,
loving you today helps more than a lot".

CHAPTER FIFTEEN

RAISING SIBLINGS

*One of the hardest things I've done is have more children.
But the best thing I've ever done is have more children.
They have each other now.*

Sunrise

You're my last baby and my new motherhood.
Here's why...
You came after everything I've been through
as a brand new mum.
As a mum of more.
As a mum who was in the trenches
and couldn't see the sunrise just yet,
even when she was up before dawn.
I learnt so much through all of that.
I loved so hard through all of that.
I am grateful for your older siblings
who were with me through all of that –
Because that's how I became ready for you.
But one thing I wasn't ready for
is how much we would all benefit from you.
All of your lessons,
passed down through your little body
that is my last.

Chapter Fifteen

I look at you, then the older ones,
and remember when they were your age and stage.
I look at you, then the older ones,
and think about what I would have done differently,
even though I was doing my best.
I look at you, then the older ones,
and see how much they get from you too.
You have re-formed my motherhood
into one of more presence, more patience,
and even more gratitude.
And that flows on to everyone.
You're my last baby.
But you have also proved to be another beginning –
The sunrise we all get to see.

Sisterhood

They are sisters.
I watch them as they play with their dolls together.
They share their clothes already,
and pick out each other's outfits.
I overhear them at night as they get into bed together
and discuss something magical in their own language.
They argue too.
But it's nothing they can't handle.
They are there for each other.
It's obvious already.
One looks up to the other.
The other looks to protect the one
who is less experienced in life.
They take up space together.
Hand in hand.
And I hope they always have this type of sisterhood.
When things change and the world shows them
what it's made of.
May they continue to find strength in each other
through everything big and small,
especially when being a woman feels hard.
Because what they have is special.
And that's what sisters are for.

Chapter Fifteen

Older siblings

I didn't have you to help me raise your siblings.
But you have helped me do it anyway.
You love them, just like I do.
You are there for them, just like I am.
And it shows.
When I'm not close, they look to you for love.
For safety.
For a home within arms.
And they find it with you.
Because you have put so much into loving them.
You have taught them things.
You have helped them through things.
You have given them something pretty remarkable.
All without being asked.

I had you for you,
and now they have you too.
An older sibling.
An undeniable guiding light.
On behalf of us all –
Thank you for everything.
On behalf of me –
Please don't forget
being an older sibling isn't your responsibility.
Being a child is.

Younger siblings

You watch as she leaves for school.
You stand with me, waving,
and then run to give her one more cuddle.
"Let's go," I say. "We'll see her soon."
When we get home you play with your toys.
It's not as loud.
You don't have to share as much.
And you get more of me.
But still, you tell me you miss her.

As we continue in our now-different days,
you point to her photos and room as we pass them.
You say her name.
"Not long now," I tell you, as I look to the clock
I've been staring at all day.
But it's been the longest day of my life.
Maybe it's been yours too.

Chapter Fifteen

We get to pick-up early.
While we wait you tell me what you are going to do
with her for the rest of the afternoon.
And when we finally see her your face lights up
at the same time as mine.
It's as if we've needed to change the lightbulb all day
but we haven't known how.
We cuddle.
And then head home.
We hear about her day,
and your day without her.
As you chat in the back seats,
and the squabbling resumes,
I think to myself –
this is hard on you too,
but what a wonderful thing to have this much love here.

Sons

I have sons, and before I became a mum,
I was under the impression that they would be
these crazy, wild, destructive creatures of nature.
And while they can be some of the time,
that's not the half of it.
They bring me heart-shaped rocks from the driveway,
beautiful flower heads from the garden,
and fluffy feathers from our walks.
They hug me tight just because,
they tell me they love me when I'm least expecting it,
and they hold my hand while I read them stories.

They ask me about my feelings,
they share their toys when I'm having a hard day,
and they want to involve me in most of their play.

These are the sons I know.
The sometimes stereotypical,
sometimes not,
always themselves,
boys.

And I am under the impression that they are perfect.

Chapter Fifteen

Daughters

I didn't realise how much my daughters would give me,
without them knowing it.
They are my strength.
My fire.
My reminders to be brave.
When I look at them I see myself
as someone new and improved.
I am in awe of them, often.
I worry about them, always.
I know that being a girl can be challenging.
It can be heavy.
It can be unfair.
I know, because I know.
I just hope they continue to breathe fire,
and be brave when being strong isn't possible.
I hope they continue to know that I am always there,
and am always proud of them,
when I can't be there to say it.
I hope that one day,
when they meet their inner children, that I am still there
with those versions of them –
on the end of their beds, embracing them,
and letting their thoughts run wild.
Because that's the goal,
when they are the dream already.

Continues with them

Siblings are built differently.
They spend their early days sharing everything.
Their toys, their time with each other, us.
So much of what they have, started with two people in love.
And what a beautiful beginning to know.
But so much of what they will always have
continues through growing up with others just like them.
Siblings are not just tied by blood, genetics,
or the same parents.
They are connected through history, shared experiences,
and being part of a family.
They are people who didn't choose each other,
but who were born into the same world
and chose to love each other,
lean on each other,
and potentially know more about each other
than any other walking and breathing beings ever will.
It starts with us,
and continues with them,
as they build an entire city from our home.

CHAPTER SIXTEEN

RAISING MYSELF

*If you feel lost in motherhood, just remember -
Your children found you exactly as they need you.
They only know this version of you.*

More than myself

I know every little detail about you.
I know how heavy you were at birth.
The time you were born.
And how long it took to hear your first cry.
I know your favourite toy.
How you prefer to be comforted.
And the way you like to eat your toast.
I know when you last went to the doctor.
How many teeth you have.
And where you keep special things.
I know what you look like when you sleep.
Where you have spots on your skin.
And when you had your last nap.
I know what makes you smile.
How to make you laugh.
And the quickest way to your heart.
I know you more than anyone.
Right now, and with pleasure –
I even know you more than myself.

Chapter Sixteen

Fun Mum

I used to be fun.
The radio reminds me of that sometimes,
as I'm taken down memory lane by a tune
I still know so well.
I don't turn it up because I can't wake the babies,
but sometimes it wakes me up enough to remember
who I used to be.
And I replay her, over and over.
We meet again this way, for short while anyway,
until she's met with her new identity,
and "mama" is called from the back seats.
I change the song to something they like and turn it up.
Together we sing along and dance to what I know
will be stuck in my head ALL DAY.
And I see how happy it makes them.
"I'm still fun," I reassure myself,
"I'm the fun mum now".

"normal"

"I can't wait to get back to normal,"
I sometimes think to myself.
But what I know is…

My body won't get back to "normal".
Because even if I lost the weight, it has carried babies,
then children and the motherload.

My mind won't get back to "normal".
Because even if I feel more mentally healthy,
I still have my heart in my head
and that changes the chemistry
of every thought pattern I entertain.

My life won't get back to "normal".
Because even if I am chasing dreams,
having time for myself, or just sleeping more,
my children will always come first
and so nothing in my day-to-day or my one day
will look like it used to.

Even if I could, I wouldn't go back to normal.
Because I am in my ever-changing,
new normal of motherhood.
And I look forward, always.

Chapter Sixteen

Light

I have been in the thick of the postpartum fog
since I became a mother.
For much of that time I've been surviving.
Half asleep, in a dark room with my babies,
waving my arms around trying to find the light switch.
It's felt out of reach.
But today –
as my last baby is suddenly much bigger,
and the stretches between sleep are much longer,
and I'm needed a little less by the others
who have grown into older versions of themselves –
I feel like I've found it.
The light is on, and I can see everything now.
And all I can say is –
What an absolutely beautiful picture to be part of.

My needs

I don't need lots of friends.
I need my family.

I don't need fancy cars and clothes.
I need my family.

I don't need a massive career.
I need my family.

And mainly, I need my health and wellness
so I can be there for as long as possible
for my family.

It's amazing what you learn when you have a family.
Nothing in my life has taught me as much
as what I now know through having a family.

And at the end of the day,
if you took everything away from me,
I'd be okay –
As long as I have my family.

CHAPTER SIXTEEN

Stop/start

Someone just asked me –
"What's so great about being a parent?"
And I didn't know how to answer.
Because I immediately became so overwhelmed
with all the great things that being a parent brings
that I didn't know where to start.
But when I did start,
I didn't know where to stop.

Wealth

I am rich.
I get to tuck my favourite people into bed each night,
knowing I keep them safe.
I get to hear little footsteps running towards our room
every morning, knowing I will get one of the first hugs.
I get to fill my day with things that matter,
knowing my family benefits from my efforts.
I am rich rich.
I get to love and be loved in a way only a parent knows.
I am filthy rich.
Parenthood has given me my life savings,
and our little family a legacy of love.

Chapter Sixteen

Something special

I don't really know what I truly enjoy anymore,
other than our family time.
I struggle to understand myself,
although more than ever I'm trying to.
And I'm not sure what I want to do with my life
when they don't need me as much.
I'm at a crossroads,
looking and searching for things I don't know I need.
I am in a space of so many unknowns
and uncertainties as a woman,
with so much meaning and purpose as a mother.
I sometimes wonder if this is a mid-life crisis,
or a motherhood one.
And I don't know the answer,
or where womanhood takes me next,
but I trust that motherhood is creating something special.
And not just for my children.

Future version

There's a version of you who you haven't met yet.
One who is a lot less tired, and more on time.
One who is just as busy, but in different ways.
One who finishes a meal and can spend more
than a few hours away without feeling guilty.
One who's house is laden with more clothes than toys,
and new words you feel too old to make sense of.
There's a version of you waiting to meet you.
She will take your hand from the depths of your early
motherhood and help you out of it when it's time.
"We will be okay," she will tell you,
as she wipes the tears from your eyes.
"We have so much to look forward to,"
her smile will say.

CHAPTER SIXTEEN

Mother

I am a mother,
with imperfections and love.
A vulnerable heart, and an oh-so-overcrowded mind.
Some days are hard. Others are blissful.
I yearn for tomorrow. But also, yesterday.
I don't know what I'm doing. And I do.
I'm stumbling, and getting up.
It's timeless here, yet I'm always late.
It's life-changing, yet I've never been more me.
I live, laugh and love,
with an undercurrent of emotional suffering.
I don't sleep, or properly eat, then repeat,
with a contentment that transcends a lifetime.
I am a mother living in contradictions.
Yet nothing,
nothing,
has ever made more sense.

CHAPTER SEVENTEEN

GROWING GAINS

Even though it can feel impossible to say "goodbye" to parts of your child, saying "hello" to parts of yourself, your children and your new type of family life through the process can be a silver lining. And it's possible to see it this way too, you know. Just when you're ready.

Chapter Seventeen

Farwell

We say goodbye.
And I don't feel ready.
Emotions get the better of me as I wave you off.
After you've moved out of sight,
I open my wallet and look at a very special photo.
Boy what we had was beautiful.
Time wasn't on our side was it?
All the little moments that got us here
were gone before we really got to sink into it.
The early days were just about us.
It was me, you and our little family against the world.
And we made it.
I'll always be so proud of us for that.
And I know what's ahead of me will take my breath away,
literally and figuratively.
But today I'm a little bit sad that we are no longer.
That we have to part ways and start over.
That it's time for something new.

Everlasting Motherhood

So, I sit and stare at the photo of us
for what seems like hours.
As the emotions move through me,
I eventually find my feet again.
And as a stranger's smile meets my eyes,
I find my perspective.
What it is to feel this way at the end
after everything we've been through.
What it is to know that being sad
because you have to say goodbye
often is testament to the incredible time that was had.
Thank you early motherhood.
You will be so dearly missed.

Chapter Seventeen

Hard truth

The reality is, I've had my turn.
As I move through early motherhood with my last baby,
I remember this.
I've had my turn to be a mother
in those precious previous moments.
I've had my turn to soak up all I can of yesterday,
even though I couldn't quite get to it all.
I've had my turn to be a lifeline, an everything,
a keeper of some of the most amazing times of my life.
I've had my turn.
I've been there and done it when they were babies.
I am ready to keep growing beside them.
I am leaving space for others to have their time
in their own early motherhood space after me.
I've had my turn, I remind myself.
Again and again,
and as many times as is needed.
Because it's a hard truth,
but a necessary one.

New meaning

What do you mean I will never witness my body carrying life inside of me again? Watch it transform before my eyes into something so powerful? Feel it be the gateway for someone's beginning?

What do you mean I will never see my children holding their brand new sibling ever again? Have my toddler ask to have a cuddle before wanting to give them back in less than 5 seconds? Get to have slow days feeding the baby while watching the older ones play or a movie as a family?

What do you mean I will never see my husband consider the features of our tiny newborn while we make the final decision on a name? Watch him proudly walk out of the hospital carrying our newest creation like it's straight out of my dreams? Have him hold the most vulnerable version of us when we get home and for a while after?

CHAPTER SEVENTEEN

What do you mean?

Do you mean that I get to see my body be strong and
resilient in different ways? That I get to see it flourish
after years of depletion, and give my children a whole
new meaning of life?

Do you mean that I get to see my babies become best friends
as they grow up together? Have more time with
each of them doing things we enjoy, because they can
meet some of their own needs now? Begin to understand,
at a deep and beautiful level, why I put myself through
the hard grind of the early years, over and over?

Do you mean that I get to see my husband more?
That we get to find our way back to each other after
what we have walked through together? That we did,
in fact, love each other all along, we were just that tired?

I think that's what I want you to mean.
Because closing the baby chapter means so much
to everyone involved.
But it gives everyone everything that follows
real meaning too.

Afterwards

I was never meant to have you as just a baby.
We were never meant to have our days together
as just you and I, when I was your everything,
and you were mine, forever and ever after that.
And while the early days with you have been nothing
short of remarkable,
while little you has been everything
I could have ever wished for,
I am meant to have every afterwards version of you too,
if you let me.
We are meant to have every afterwards version
of our days together where we both change
but our love stays the same, if we are both that lucky.
I hope you know that you are more than the baby years
or the booties that no longer fit.
I hope you know that the photos of us
when we were fresher versions of ourselves
are not the only ones that really matter.
I hope you never forget –
you are my before,
my during,
and always my happily ever after.
And I can't wait to keep loving you forever.

Chapter Seventeen

Me to you

When I say I want to give you the world,
I don't necessarily mean the disposable things,
or even money.
I mainly mean I want to give you kindness,
empathy and strength.
An emotional security that doesn't have a use by date,
and a trust in yourself.
I want to give you:
the inner knowing that you can do anything,
all love I possibly can,
and an always-Mum.
I want to give you the best I know,
and the even better I'm still trying to find.
Because you have given me the world,
by simply being born.

Cool Mum

Maybe I'm a "cool mum"
just not the usual "type".
I hardly know the latest trends,
or follow the teenage hype.

And I don't have all the answers.
Sometimes I feel quite lost.
And there are days where my exhaustion
comes at more of a cost.

But I work to get it right
and I work harder after mistakes.
I am always giving, always evolving,
doing whatever my better takes.

I listen to their needs.
I put time into their thoughts.
I show up when they need it,
as their unwavering support.

Chapter Seventeen

I let them have compassion.
I lead them into grace.
I remind them I'm always here
when they need a little space.

I speak to them with kindness.
I apologise when I'm wrong.
I tell them I love them every day,
and show them that they belong.

And I know that they don't see it.
I'm not their definition of "cool".
I'm their same old, everyday mum,
and I make all the rules.

But one day when they're older,
and they've grown into their skin –
maybe they'll see the benefits
of what I've truly given them.

Maybe I'll be the "cool mum"
for doing things my way.
Maybe they'll call me the trendy one
for being their everyday.

All grown up

I can wait, you know.
I can wait until you are bigger than me.
I can wait until I have to pick you up early in the morning.
I can wait until you tell me unkind things
in the heat of the moment.
Watching you grow up isn't easy, you know.
But I'm not scared.
I can't wait to be there for you when you still need me.
I can't wait to be your safe space when you are all grown up.
I've got you.
Time won't tell.
My love already does.

Chapter Seventeen

Gift

You were the first to have babies.
Maybe of your siblings.
Maybe of your friends.
And so you entered everything without knowing anything.
Every first felt huge because you were blind.
And every last felt lonely because you were alone.
You paved the way for the others.
And what a brave thing to do.
You were constantly out of your comfort zone,
without others to share in it with.
The joy and the hardships harboured inside,
waiting for others to catch up.
But look at you go.
You continue to make it.
And now you have so much to give.
You can pass down more than the hand-me-downs.
There's knowledge, experience,
and such wisdom that comes
from having to learn the hard way
if others want to hear it.
I know it hasn't always been easy.
I know you will continue to feel alone sometimes
as your babies grow.
But you are a gift.
Not only to your children,
but to the others following in your footsteps too.

Reminders that stand the test of time

Motherhood doesn't age you. It matures you.

For better or worse you can be the most memorable person your children know.

It doesn't get easier. It just gets different.
But you adapt and get stronger through every part.

No one else knows how much you put into your family. Let that be your biggest secret.

You set the tone for your home. The work you put in will be in your children's playlists forever.

CHAPTER EIGHTEEN

LOOKING BACK

*The benefit of hindsight, in motherhood,
is not just what you would do if you got a next time.
It's that you can remember what it was like to be there at all.*

The chance

Somewhere along the way
my café coffees turned into takeaways,
my style turned into comfort,
and my punctual turned into late.

Somewhere along the way
my quiet turned into chaos,
my days turned into nights,
and my payslips turned into presence.

Somewhere along the way
my tidy turned into lived-in,
my size turned into caring less,
and my purpose turned into them.

Chapter Eighteen

Somewhere along the way
losing myself turned into finding myself,
not knowing myself turned into understanding myself,
and not recognising my reflection
turned into meeting myself again at the exact right time.

Somewhere along the way
my life turned into love,
my love turned into my strength,
and my strength turned into something
completely unstoppable.

Somewhere along the way
I found it all in one place,
I turned it into my own story,
and I never stopped writing it.

Because somewhere along the way it happened.
I got the chance to be someone's mum.
And I wouldn't have it any other way.

Speed of time

To everyone else –
Suddenly you have a baby.
Then a toddler.
Then a pre-schooler.
Then a school kid.

To you –
You have lived,
loved,
and endured
every beautiful,
hard,
profound,
slow-long day
of the last few years.
Until all of a sudden,
you wonder where every second of it went.

Chapter Eighteen

This too shall pass

When I was in it –
I thought pregnancy would go on forever.
I thought the sleepless nights would go on forever.
I thought the toddler tantrums would go on forever
and ever after that.
But now I'm out of it –
I can look back knowing that it was all temporary.
Now that I'm out of it –
facing new temporary stages of something else
with a baby who is nowhere near as small
as what seems like only yesterday,
I know how fast it really goes.
And that's a feeling that will last forever.

Would I?

If I could go back in time, would I?
Would I get up every few hours
knowing tomorrow night won't be any different for a while?
Would I watch myself transform into someone
who I barely recognise – for better,
even though it sometimes feels for worse?
Would I miss out on things, be late for things,
and overthink every little thing until I know no different?
Would I forget myself over and over
and then spend years trying to remember?
Would I struggle through for a while knowing it's temporary,
but not knowing when it gets easier?
Would I?
The answer is yes.
A million times yes.
I would, if I could, in a heartbeat –
Because there is so much more to it than every hard part,
even if that can be hard to see when you are in it.
I would do anything to hold their bodies of yesterday,
which I struggle to remember today.
I would do anything to hear the words they used to
mispronounce, just to be sure of the ones they were.
I would do anything to wash their smaller outfits again,
to know that there is still more time with them at that stage.
Because I'm forgetting now,
and the photos aren't enough.

Chapter Eighteen

Made to last

I wish someone had told me that there's more to
look forward to than the baby stage.
That the cuteness doesn't end, it just looks different.
That the newborn scrunches may turn into
longer-awaited hugs, and the onesies may turn into
multiple outfit changes per day, but the love will always
remain constant.

I wish someone had told me that there's more to motherhood
than changing nappies, and waking in the night.
That this is some of life's most important work,
but it's not the only definition of a mother's mission.
That baby chats turn into life-long discussions
that really matter.
That connection is sought just as much, if not even more,
just in different ways.
That as your child moves into new stages, so do you,
because you do not have a best before date.

Everlasting Motherhood

I wish someone had told me that there will always be
more to me in my motherhood than the mother of yesterday.
That the relentlessness and exhaustion is still there,
yes, but you have more energy for other parts
of yourself and your motherhood too.
That as more time for you comes,
more time for them comes too.
That as you sleep more, you have space to choose
the mother you want to be, and as you lose
some of the physically challenging parts,
your child gains more of the best parts of you.

I wish that someone, anyone, had told me
that a mother's heart doesn't stop when her baby
is no longer a baby.
Because it was made to outlast tiny fingers and toes,
toddler cuddles, pre-schooler firsts and those few initial years
that will always hold a special place within you.

I wish someone had told me.
Because I believe it now.
With my whole heart.

Chapter Eighteen

POV: They're no longer little

When you were little, I used to hug you in the morning before we did anything else. Sometimes I would lift you up and spin you 'round and 'round first. I knew you liked that best.

When you were little, I used to lay with you before you fell asleep. I loved having some one-on-one quiet time with you, in what sometimes felt like the first time that day.

When you were little, I used to tell you I loved you every single day, and often more than once. We used to compete about who loved each other more, and kept going until someone felt like they won.

When you were little, I used to make "whatever you want" dinners when I was tired. I never once regretted that, as you ate and asked for more while I heard about your day. They turned out to be some of my favourite mealtimes.

Everlasting Motherhood

When you were little, I used to play your favourite music and watch you dance in the living room. Sometimes I danced too. We laughed and were silly, and for a moment I felt like a child again too.

When you were little there was so much joy in our home, but I was surviving. I tried and tried and tried some more to be the mother you needed in all the ways I could be, but sometimes I couldn't. You were the only definition of perfect then.

But you are no longer little, although as perfect as ever. And I'm no longer just surviving, although as imperfect as I always could be. And yet, I still remember the days when you were little like yesterday.

Thank you for those days.
They give me so much to smile about, even now.

Chapter Eighteen

Unstoppable

Whenever I am feeling weak,
I will think back to that moment in time
when I was the most powerful I have ever been.
I will let myself remember –
How much I endured to get there,
how much I kept pushing when it felt impossible,
how much of every second of the pain
was worth it in the end.
I'll be there again,
in that room,
holding my babies for the very first time.
Because when I'm there,
back in my power,
NOTHING can stop me.

Knowing

To be pregnant –
is to have your entire world living inside of you.

To have a child in your arms –
is to have your entire heart living outside of your chest.

To be a mother –
is without question,
the most amazingly terrifying ride of your life.

CHAPTER NINETEEN

EVERLASTING MOTHERHOOD

*The second half of my life began when I entered motherhood.
And I will remain in this half,
while inviting other stages in to join,
for the rest of my life.*

Opportunity

Sometimes I get caught up in the past.
I think about all the things I don't have anymore.
Like the stirs inside of my belly,
or the tiny baby sleeping on my chest.
Like the little things that felt so big at the time,
or the moments that made my children of yesterday
so special.
It can feel like the photos don't do the memories justice.
Or that the memories don't give the previous moments
a longevity of life.
And sometimes I do just need to feel sorry for myself because
of that.
But generally speaking, I don't want to be the victim
of that mentality.
I can be sad and see only the things that make me feel low.
I can feel mediocre and try not to think too much
about anything to protect my feelings.
Or I can be excited and ready to flourish.

Chapter Nineteen

I am in charge of how I see things.
It's a choice I can make.
And the truth is that I've loved every stage of my children.
Everything new and different surprises me in the best way.
What's to say that won't continue?
What's to say that I can't wake up every day
knowing there's no more of my children yesterday,
but so many more of them today, tomorrow and next year?
With each new day there's someone new
I can't wait to meet.
And time, even if it does move fast,
gives me that opportunity.

Always

Even when I'm not carrying my children,
I am carrying them.
I carry them in my mind -
In every thought about what they need.
In every worry about what could happen.
In every reminder of what we are doing tomorrow.
I carry them in my heart -
In every heaviness when something goes wrong.
In every warmth when everything goes right.
In every skipped beat when I have to trust the process.
I carry my children in every fibre of my being.
When they are not with me, they are.
They are with me, always.

Chapter Nineteen

Forever home

You are with me now.
No matter the issue, you come to me –
without hesitation.
No questions asked.

We sit in your room, on the floor,
or outside on the patio, and cuddle.
You tell me your problems however you can.
Sometimes with words.
Sometimes with tears.
Sometimes without much more than a sigh into my chest.
"I'm here," I tell you.

This home holds many of these memories now.
It has been witness to emotional safety
and unconditional love.
And this is something I don't want to change.

As you grow, and you feel your problems can't be fixed
by a kiss from me, or a hug that doesn't fit the same,
I want you to know you can always come home anyway.

Everlasting Motherhood

You can sit in the pantry and sob with the treats –
You'll always know where I keep them.
You can lie in your old bed and come down for dinner
when you are ready –
I'll be waiting.
You can come and go when you need to and stay for as long
you want –
It's not invite-only here.

I will always be here for you,
if not in this home, in another.
And I'll always offer the hugs, treats
and emotional safety I try so hard to give you now,
even if you don't want these things then.

And you don't owe me anything in this life,
but if I can ask just one thing
it would be that no matter the issue, worry, or life event –
you know that you can always come back to me.
Without hesitation.
No questions asked.

Because I'm here.
And I always will be.
Because for you,
a seat in my life will always be reserved.

Please –
Just come home.

Chapter Nineteen

Stay

I study and become what I want to be.
But I can leave that and change paths.

I try new things and choose what I want to pursue
because they bring me joy.
But some things suit certain periods of my life better
than others.

I meet people and decide I want to spend more time
with them.
But that doesn't always mean our relationships last,
because people come and go.

But when I grew and birthed each of my children,
I became a mother to someone.

And through everything that life throws at me,
through every new opportunity I choose to take,
through everyone I take a chance on –
The mother in me will stay.

Because once in motherhood,
always in motherhood.
Once a mother,
forever I'll be.

Destination heart

If my heart were a place –
It would be wherever you are,
with roads taking me back to the best of our memories.

The rooms would be filled with your favourite things,
and there would always be enough space to keep it all.

The walls would be painted in warm colours
and the garden would be a haven of beauty,
because that's how you make me feel.

It would smell of freshly baked pancakes on a
Sunday morning, and your scent every day of the week,
as the sweetness of it all continued to linger.

The sound of your laughter would fill every corner,
and I would always be able to hear the different voices
of your childhood.

If my heart were a place –
It would be all of you,
in our little moments,
found in one place.
And it would never,
ever,
stop beating.

Chapter Nineteen

Take a bow

I am my children's "Behind The Scenes".
I make sure everything runs as smoothly as possible.
I am there when it doesn't.
I get it all back on track so no one thinks otherwise.
And while others will clap at their achievements,
I clap the loudest.
Because this isn't about me.
It never was.
It is about making sure they have everything they need
so that they can stand in front of life,
be proud of who they are,
and take a bow before the curtains close.

My children

I hope you find the love you deserve
as you move past mine,
but if,
for whatever reason,
you don't,
I hope mine is enough
to make you feel
unconditionally loveable forever.

Chapter Nineteen

Best parts

I met an older mother recently.
When she found out I was a mother too,
she immediately told me about her own children,
and grandchildren.
She told me how old they are.
Where they live.
What they do.
She was smiling the entire time.
And when I told her about mine,
she smiled some more.
Almost all of our discussion was around our babies,
young and grown.
And I guess it goes to show –
Mothers never stop talking about their children.
For many –
Their children and families will always be
the first stories they wish to share,
even if they have many other amazing things in their lives.
For many –
Motherhood isn't their whole identity,
but their children will always be
one of the best parts of it.

Until the end

One day you will be there as they enjoy their favourite meal that you used to make them, and the company they've continued to keep.
One day you will be there as they receive an accolade they've worked so hard on, and they thank you in their speech.
One day you will be there as they parent their own children, and realise they still need parenting too.
Or maybe you won't.
Maybe your time runs out early and they have to do it without you.
Or maybe you live until the end and they live longer as you hoped.
Either way, please know…
You won't always be here.
But you will always be there.
Because you were there from day one.
And every day after that.
Because when you are someone's first example of showing up,
and their continued example of being there –
They will remember you until the end.

CHAPTER NINETEEN

Remember when

You will always be someone's "do you remember when?"
Do you remember when she used to take us to get ice creams
and almost always finished ours?

Do you remember when she let us stay up that little bit
later just so we got to talk to her that little bit longer?

Do you remember when she used to rush around
getting herself ready last, while we all asked her to
hurry up from the car?

You will always be someone's "do you remember that time?"

Do you remember that time she burnt the potatoes so
badly that the house nearly caught on fire?

Do you remember that time we found her secret stash
of sweets in the laundry cupboard?

Do you remember that time she fell asleep while reading
us a story and the book nearly broke her nose?

Everlasting Motherhood

You will always be someone's "do you remember how?"

Do you remember how she used to call us all the
wrong names, and sometimes even the pet's?

Do you remember how she used to put little
hand-written notes in our lunchboxes when we were
having a hard time?

Do you remember how she used to call us and
leave endless voicemails rather than just texting us?

You will always be someone's "do you remember?"

Do you remember those holidays where we came home
to surprise her and she said it made her whole year?

Do you remember that Christmas we watched all of our
old family videos that she had saved for all that time?

Do you remember her birthday party last year where
she asked us to stay the night like we used to?

And even though it's hard to see it at the time,
you are making someone's "I remember" moments
time and time again.
And not just during your motherhood,
but for a long while after it too.

Motherhood is waking up and realising –
It wasn't just a dream.
It is an everlasting part of life.

You can find me on social media at:

@Wordsof_Emmaheaphy

@Wordsofemmaheaphy

www.ingramcontent.com/pod-product-compliance
Lightning Source LLC
Chambersburg PA
CBHW020837160426
43192CB00007B/691